Webber® Core Curriculum Vocabulary Cards Fun Sheets

Level Two

Research-Based Vocabulary

Written & Illustrated by the Super Duper® Staff

Copyright © 2012 by SUPER DUPER® PUBLICATIONS,
a division of Super Duper®, Inc. All rights reserved.

Copyright ©2012, SUPER DUPER® PUBLICATIONS, a division of Super Duper®, Inc. All rights reserved. Permission is granted for the user to reproduce the material contained herein in limited form for classroom use only. Reproduction of this material for an entire school or school system is strictly prohibited. No part of this material may be reproduced (except as noted above), stored in a retrieval system, or transmitted in any form or by any means (mechanically, electronically, recording, web, etc.) without the prior written consent and approval of Super Duper® Publications.

Printed in the United States

ISBN 978-1-60723-045-8

Super Duper® Publications
www.superduperinc.com
1-800-277-8737

Introduction

Webber® Core Curriculum Vocabulary Cards Fun Sheets – Level Two doubles the opportunities for teaching vocabulary available in the original *Webber® Core Curriculum Vocabulary Cards*! This reproducible companion workbook has 104 pages of activities to help teach and reinforce the 100 research-based vocabulary words presented in the *Webber® Core Curriculum Cards – Level Two*. Each subject area (Language Arts, Math, Science, and Social Studies) contains 25 core curriculum words students need to know in order to experience confidence and success in the classroom.

Each activity page helps students build confidence in their vocabulary skills, encourages following directions, and improves their comprehension of these basic, but critical, terms. Regular classroom teachers, speech-language pathologists, reading specialists, and special education teachers can use this book **with or without** the *Core Curriculum Cards* in one-on-one therapy sessions, with small groups, or with an entire class.

Each subject area has activities that include

- Definition Match-Up
- Comprehension
- WH Questions
- Vocabulary in Context
- Categories
- Phonological Awareness
- Spelling
- Writing Definitions

Webber® Core Curriculum Vocabulary Cards Fun Sheets – Level Two is ideal for students in Title 1, ESL, or Head Start programs as well as students with special needs. Use the worksheets for extension activities, homework, or simple assessments.

Table of Contents

Parent/Helper Letter vi

Language Arts 1–26
Definition Match-Up.. 1–3
Comprehension... 4–6
WH Questions 7–9
Vocabulary in Context 10–12
Categories 13–15
Phonological Awareness 16–19
Spelling 20–22
Writing Definitions 23–26

Math.. 27–52
Definition Match-Up... 27–29
Comprehension 30–32
WH Questions 33–35
Vocabulary in Context 36–38
Categories 39–41
Phonological Awareness 42–45
Spelling 46–48
Writing Definitions 49–52

Science 53–78
Definition Match-Up... 53–55
Comprehension 56–58
WH Questions 59–61
Vocabulary in Context 62–64
Categories 65–67
Phonological Awareness 68–71
Spelling 72–74
Writing Definitions 75–78

Social Studies 79–104
Definition Match-Up... 79–81
Comprehension 82–84
WH Questions 85–87
Vocabulary in Context 88–90
Categories 91–93
Phonological Awareness 94–97
Spelling 98–100
Writing Definitions 101–104

Parent/Helper Letter

Date: _____

Dear Parent/Helper:

Your child is currently working on _____.

The attached worksheet(s) will help your child practice and reinforce skills reviewed in the classroom.

☐ After you complete these exercises with your child, please sign and return them by _____.

☐ Please complete these exercises with your child. You do not need to return them to me.

☐ _____
_____
_____

Thank you for your support.

_____ _____
Teacher/Speech-Language Pathologist Parent/Helper Signature

Language Arts – Definition Match-Up

Directions: Draw a line from the definition in Column A to the word that matches it in Column B. Read/Say the definition and its matching vocabulary word aloud.

A

Column A	Column B
Tuesday = Tues. / Virginia = VA / Mister = Mr. / Doctor = Dr. — This is a shorter version of one or more words.	biography
 This is the way you look or speak that shows how you are feeling.	compound word
cow + boy = cowboy / basket + ball = basketball / rain + bow = rainbow / skate + board = skateboard / cup + cake = cupcake / jelly + fish = jellyfish / butter + fly = butterfly — This is a combination of two words to make one word.	abbreviation
 This is what a story is about.	sequence
 This is a story about a person's life.	main idea
 This is the order of events in a story.	expression

_____ _____ _____
Name   Date   Helper

Language Arts – Star Match-Up

Directions: Cut out the definitions at the bottom of the page. Shuffle the definitions and place them facedown. Have the students take turns reading the definitions and placing them next to the correct pictures. The first player to find the star is the winner.

 comprehension

 voice

 contrast

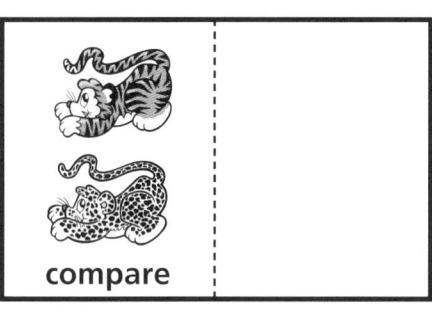 compare

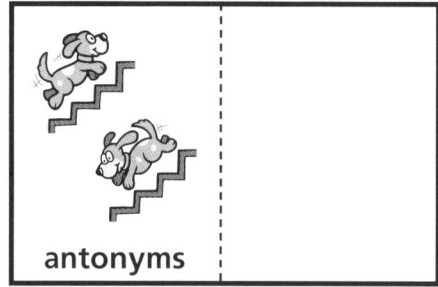 antonyms

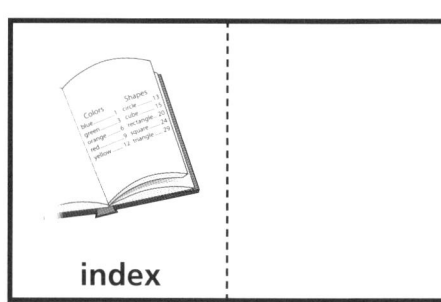 index

pretty = beautiful
baby = infant
below = under
always = forever
synonyms

will + not = won't
let + us = let's
you + are = you're
I + am = I'm
we + are = we're
it + has = it's
where + is = where's
contraction

pre • view = preview (before)
re • turn = return (back)
un • do = undo (not)
prefix

| These are words that have opposite meanings. | This is the beginning part of a word that has its own meaning. | These are words that have the same meaning. | This is when you find the similarities between things. | This is understanding what you read or hear. |
| ★ | This is a word for the way you express yourself in writing. | This is when you find the differences between things. | This is the section at the end of a book that lists topics and page numbers. | This is a word that combines two words into one by using an apostrophe. |

Name _____ Date _____ Helper _____

Language Arts – Treasure Chest Match-Up

Directions: Cut out the definitions at the bottom of the page. Shuffle the definitions and place them facedown. Have the students take turns reading the definitions and placing them next to the correct pictures. The first player to find the treasure chest is the winner.

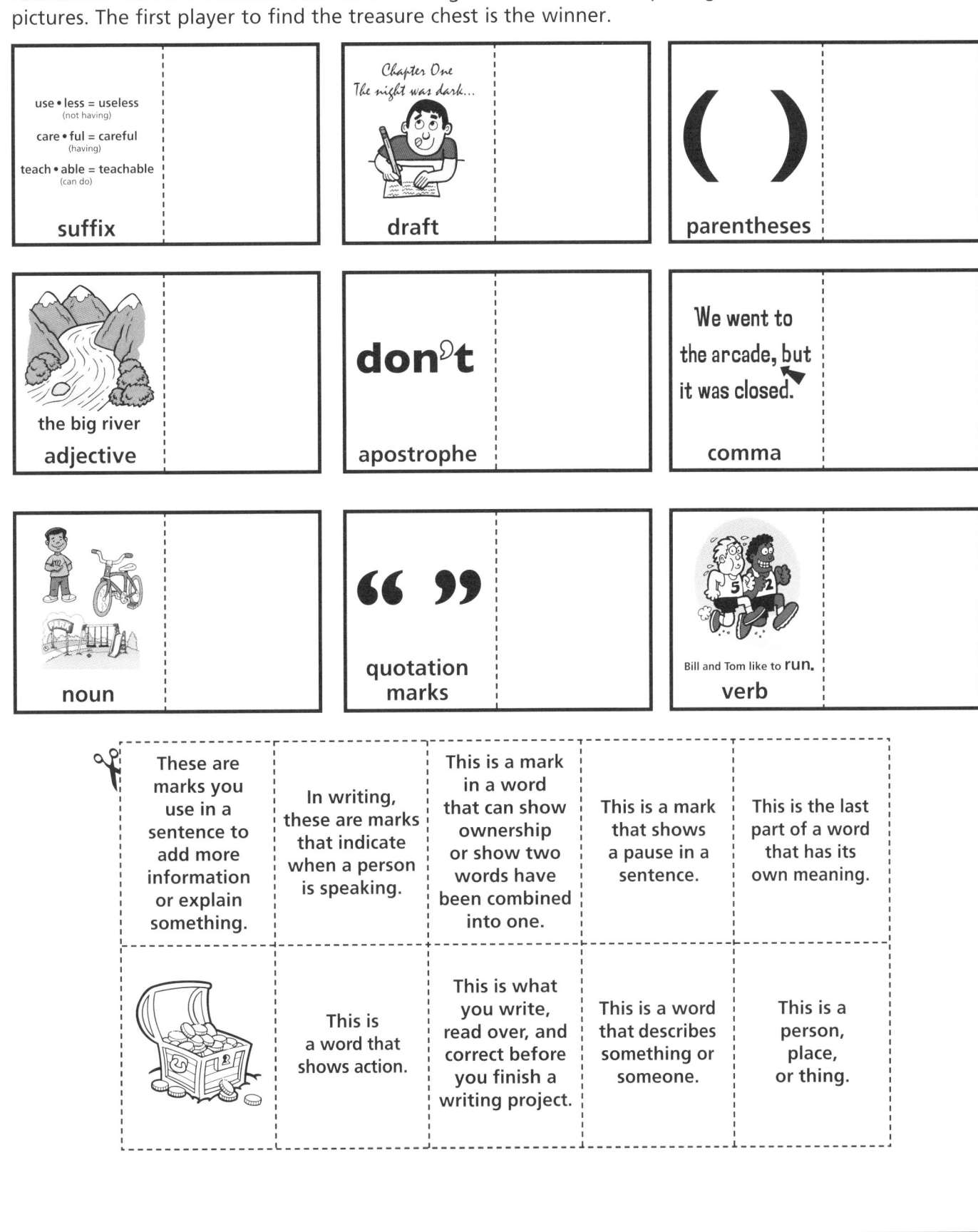

Language Arts – What's the Correct Meaning?

Directions: Read each sentence. Circle the picture and definition on the right that have the correct meaning for the word in bold.

1. The **dictionary** says that a "pram" is a baby carriage.

    This is what you write, read over, and correct before you finish a writing project.

    This is a book that spells and defines many words.

---

2. You can tell by Tim's **expression** that he is not happy.

    This is the way you look or speak that shows how you are feeling.

    This is a word that describes something or someone.

---

3. The **suffix** tells me that beautiful means "having beauty."

   pre • view = preview (before)
   re • turn = return (back)
   un • do = undo (not)
   This is the beginning part of a word that has its own meaning.

   use • less = useless (not having)
   care • ful = careful (having)
   teach • able = teachable (can do)
   This is the last part of a word that has its own meaning.

---

4. When I read the first **draft** of my story, I had to make some corrections.

    This is what you write, read over, and correct before you finish a writing project.

    This is when you find the differences between things.

---

5. Bett put her phone number in **parentheses** at the bottom of her email.

    In writing, these are marks that indicate when a person is speaking.

   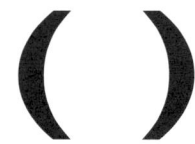 These are marks you use in a sentence to add more information or explain something.

---

6. Shel Silverstein's writings have a gentle and kind **voice**.

    This is a word for the way you express yourself in writing.

    This is the order of events in a story.

Name _____ Date _____ Helper _____

Language Arts – What's the Correct Meaning?

Directions: Read each sentence. Circle the picture and definition on the right that have the correct meaning for the word in bold.

1. There is a sharp **contrast** between the characters in the story.

    This is when you find the similarities between things.

    This is when you find the differences between things.

---

2. The events in Sue's story are not in the correct **sequence**.

    This is the order of events in a story.

    This is the section at the end of a book that lists topics and page numbers.

---

3. After the teacher told us the **main idea** of the story, we all wanted to read it.

    This is what a story is about.

    This is a story about a person's life.

---

4. When a recipe tells me to "preheat" the oven, the **prefix** "pre" tells me to heat the oven before baking.

   pre • view = preview (before)
   re • turn = return (back)
   un • do = undo (not)
   This is the beginning part of a word that has its own meaning.

   use • less = useless (not having)
   care • ful = careful (having)
   teach • able = teachable (can do)
   This is the last part of a word that has its own meaning.

---

5. The words "hot" and "cold" are **antonyms**.

   pretty = beautiful
   baby = infant
   below = under
   always = forever
   These are words that have the same meaning.

    These are words that have opposite meanings.

---

6. The **contraction** "hadn't" means "had not."

    This is a mark in a word that can show ownership or show two words have been combined into one.

   will + not = won't
   let + us = let's
   you + are = you're
   I + am = I'm
   we + are = we're
   it + has = it's
   where + is = where's
   This is a word that combines two words into one by using an apostrophe.

Name _____ Date _____ Helper _____

Language Arts – What's the Correct Meaning?

Directions: Read each sentence. Circle the picture and definition on the right that have the correct meaning for the word in bold.

1. Our teacher read us a **biography** about George Washington.	 This is a story about a person's life.	 This is understanding what you read or hear.
2. Barnyard is a **compound word** that means the yard area around the barn.	cow + boy = cowboy basket + ball = basketball rain + bow = rainbow skate + board = skateboard cup + cake = cupcake jelly + fish = jellyfish butter + fly = butterfly This is a combination of two words to make one word.	will + not = won't let + us = let's you + are = you're I + am = I'm we + are = we're it + has = it's where + is = where's This is a word that combines two words into one by using an apostrophe.
3. It's easy to **compare** the twins Bill and Will because they're so much alike.	 This is when you find the differences between things.	 This is when you find the similarities between things.
4. You'll find the page numbers in the **index**.	 This is the section at the end of a book that lists topics and page numbers.	 This is a book that spells and defines many words.
5. The words "mad" and "angry" are **synonyms**.	pretty = beautiful baby = infant below = under always = forever These are words that have the same meaning.	 These are words that have opposite meanings.
6. All contractions must use an **apostrophe**.	 This is a mark in a word that can show ownership or show two words have been combined into one.	We went to the arcade, but it was closed. This is a mark that shows a pause in a sentence.

_____ _____ _____
Name Date Helper

Language Arts – Answer It!

Directions: Read each question. Then, put an X on the letter next to the picture and vocabulary word that best answers the question.

1. Which mark shows ownership or combines two words into one?

    We went to the arcade, but it was closed.
   comma

    don't
   apostrophe

2. Which is the last part of a word that has its own meaning?

   pre • view = preview (before)
   re • turn = return (back)
   un • do = undo (not)
   prefix

   use • less = useless (not having)
   care • ful = careful (having)
   teach • able = teachable (can do)
   suffix

3. Which tells the order of events in a story?

   contrast

   sequence

4. What describes the words "near" and "far"?

   pretty = beautiful
   baby = infant
   below = under
   always = forever
   synonyms

   antonyms

5. What shows other people how you are feeling?

   biography

   expression

6. Which spells and defines words?

   index

   dictionary

_____   _____   _____
Name   Date   Helper

Language Arts – Answer It!

Directions: Read each question. Then, put an X on the letter next to the picture and vocabulary word that best answers the question.

1. What are words with similar meanings?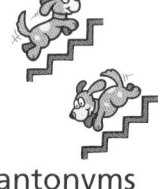

                                                                    antonyms   synonyms

---

2. What kind of word describes a noun?

                                                                     verb   adjective

---

3. Which shows a pause in a sentence?

                                                                comma   parentheses

---

4. What names a person, place, or thing?

                                                                    verb   noun

---

5. What shows that a person is speaking in a story?

                                              quotation marks   expression

---

6. Which names an action that something or someone is doing?

                                                             prefix   verb

---

Name _____ Date _____ Helper _____

Language Arts – Answer It!

Directions: Read each question. Then put an X on the letter next to the picture and vocabulary word that best answers the question.

---

1. What is understanding what you read and hear?

             comprehension   expression

---

2. What is a shortened name for something?

   will + not = won't
   let + us = let's
   you + are = you're
   I + am = I'm
   we + are = we're
   it + has = it's
   where + is = where's
   contraction

   Tuesday = Tues.
   Virginia = VA
   Mister = Mr.
   Doctor = Dr.
   abbreviation

---

3. Which book tells the story of someone's life?

        biography   dictionary

---

4. Which beginning part of a word has its own meaning?

   pre • view = preview (before)
   re • turn = return (back)
   un • do = undo (not)
   prefix

   use • less = useless (not having)
   care • ful = careful (having)
   teach • able = teachable (can do)
   suffix

---

5. What do I write and correct before making a final copy?

        draft   sequence

---

6. What is the way you express your feelings in your writing?

       B

        contrast   voice

Name   Date   Helper

Language Arts – Sentence Completion

Directions: Read each sentence below. Complete each sentence using a vocabulary word from the Word/Picture Bank. Write the word in the blank.

Word/Picture Bank

compound word	contrast	main idea	compare	contraction
expression	voice	parentheses	biography	comprehension

1. The _____ in Sara's writing expresses her passion in caring for dogs and cats.

2. Clint and Mark are so different, there are no ways to _____ them.

3. When I read the _____ of the story, I knew what it was going to be about.

4. What words form the _____ "shouldn't"?

5. The _____ on Amy's face was one of surprised.

6. A _____ about Dr. Seuss will be in stores next week.

7. It's easy to figure out the meaning of the _____ "campground."

8. The vocabulary word in each sentence has its definition in _____ beside it.

9. Our assignment was to _____ the elephant and the mouse.

10. At the end of each story, we will answer _____ questions about the characters and events.

_____   _____   _____
Name   Date   Helper

Language Arts – Sentence Completion

Directions: Read each sentence below. Complete each sentence using a vocabulary word from the Word/Picture Bank. Write the word in the blank.

Word/Picture Bank

suffix	draft	dictionary	abbreviation	synonyms
adjective	comma	noun	quotation marks	verb

1. The _____ tells that the word "tearful" means full of or having tears.

2. Which _____ describes me better, happy or funny?

3. How does the _____ define the word "complex"?

4. Jeff wrote the first _____ of his science report in less than an hour.

5. What is the _____ for South Carolina?

6. A simple sentence has a _____ and a verb.

7. You must use _____ to show exactly what someone said at the meeting.

8. Our assignment was to list every _____ that people in the picture were doing, like running and playing.

9. Laugh, giggle, and chuckle are _____ of each other.

10. You must use a _____ between the name of the city and state.

_____   _____   _____
Name   Date   Helper

Language Arts – Sentence Completion

Directions: Read each sentence below. Complete each sentence using a vocabulary word from the Word/Picture Bank. Write the word in the blank.

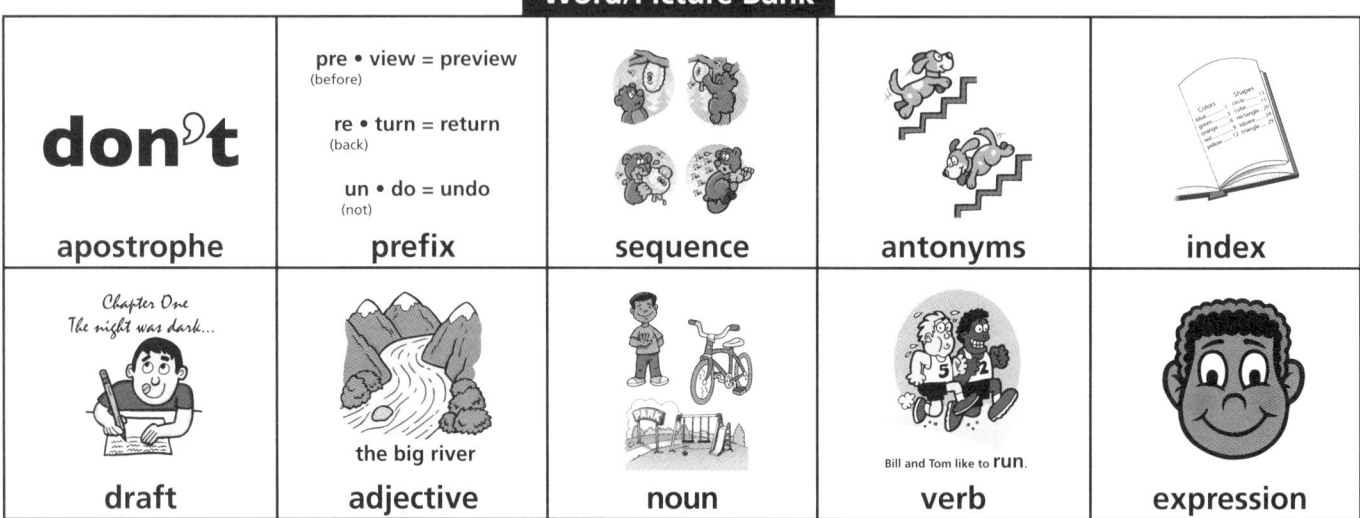

1. The _____ "re-" tells you that "reheat" means to heat again.

2. When writing a contraction, replace the missing letter or letters with an _____.

3. What _____ best describes the sun?

4. Missy's _____ lets us know that she is mad.

5. Find "rainforest" in the _____ and tell us the page number where we can find it.

6. The words "up" and "down" are _____.

7. For a story to make sense, the events must be in _____.

8. Mrs. Sims told us to write a _____ for our essay on recycling.

9. The teacher challenged us to write a list of every _____ we see in the room.

10. A _____ tells us the action happening in a sentence.

_____   _____   _____
        Name   Date   Helper

Language Arts – Which Ones Belong Together?

Directions: Cut out the three pictures in Row 1. Glue the two pictures that go together in the empty boxes on the left. Tell why the two pictures go together. Complete the page one row at a time.

1.

don't **apostrophe**	will + not = won't let + us = let's you + are = you're I + am = I'm we + are = we're it + has = it's where + is = where's **contraction**	**comprehension**

2.

sequence	pre • view = preview (before) re • turn = return (back) un • do = undo (not) **prefix**	use • less = useless (not having) care • ful = careful (having) teach • able = teachable (can do) **suffix**

3.

antonyms	pretty = beautiful baby = infant below = under always = forever **synonyms**	**index**

4.

voice	**compare**	**contrast**

5.

noun	Bill and Tom like to run. **verb**	Chapter One The night was dark... **draft**

6.

expression	will + not = won't let + us = let's you + are = you're I + am = I'm we + are = we're it + has = it's where + is = where's **contraction**	cow + boy = cowboy basket + ball = basketball rain + bow = rainbow skate + board = skateboard cup + cake = cupcake jelly + fish = jellyfish butter + fly = butterfly **compound word**

_____ _____ _____
Name   Date   Helper

Language Arts – Which Doesn't Belong?

Directions: Read/Listen carefully to each group of words. Mark an X through the word that doesn't belong. Tell how the other words relate to each other.

1. main idea, index, sequence, comma

2. apostrophe, contrast, quotation marks, parentheses

the big river

3. quotation marks, comma, apostrophe, noun

4. main idea, draft, sequence, contrast

5. noun, parentheses, compound word, verb

6. prefix, suffix, compound word, voice

7. biography, abbreviation, contraction, compound word

8. dictionary, index, biography, verb

9. parentheses, apostrophe, comma, contrast

10. verb, noun, index, adjective

Bill and Tom like to run.

_____   _____   _____
        Name   Date   Helper

Language Arts – Which Doesn't Belong?

Directions: Put an X through the picture in each row that doesn't belong. Tell why the other two pictures belong together.

1.  antonyms  | biography | pretty = beautiful / baby = infant / below = under / always = forever — synonyms

2. We went to the arcade, but it was closed. — comma | 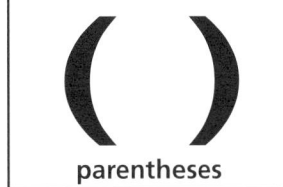 parentheses | will + not = won't / let + us = let's / you + are = you're / I + am = I'm / we + are = we're / it + has = it's / where + is = where's — contraction

3. pre • view = preview (before) / re • turn = return (back) / un • do = undo (not) — prefix |  main idea | use • less = useless (not having) / care • ful = careful (having) / teach • able = teachable (can do) — suffix

4. 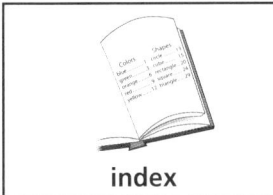 index |  noun |  Bill and Tom like to run. verb

5.  contrast |  Chapter One The night was dark... draft | 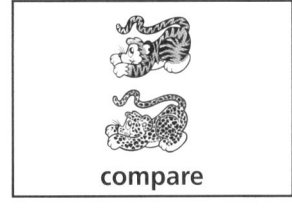 compare

6.  expression |  The dog buried his bone in the backyard. Then he began... voice |  sequence

_____   _____   _____
Name   Date   Helper

Language Arts – Say It, Paste It - Initial

Directions: Have the student cut out the pictures at the bottom of the page. The helper names a picture aloud, then the student glues/tapes or places it on the big picture with the same *beginning* sound.

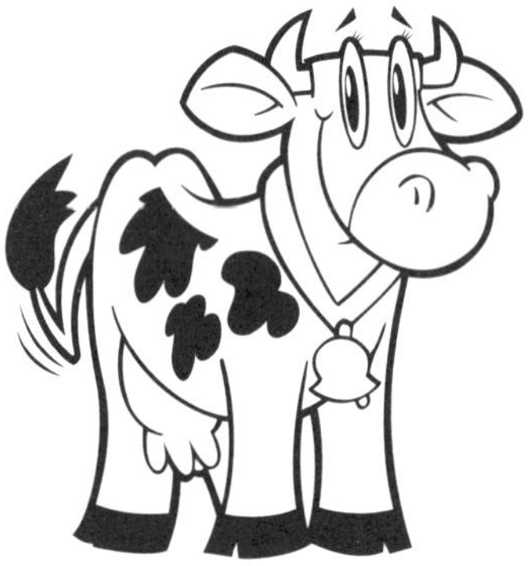

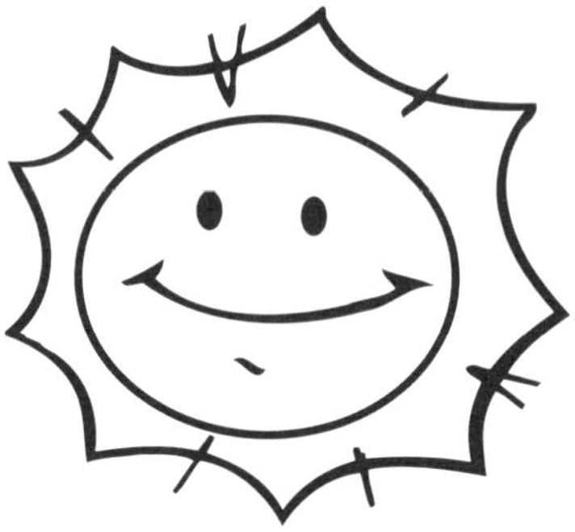

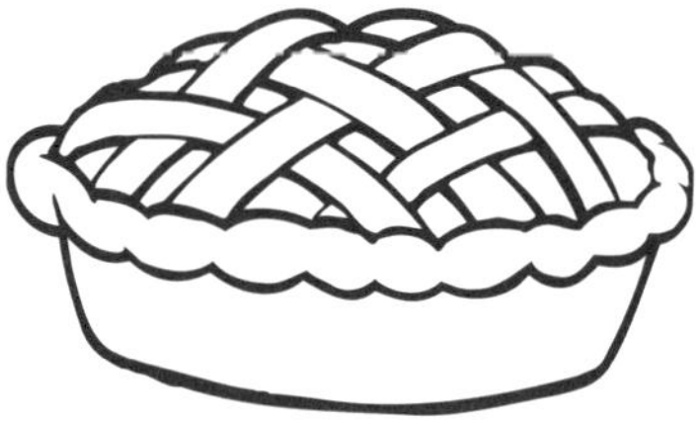

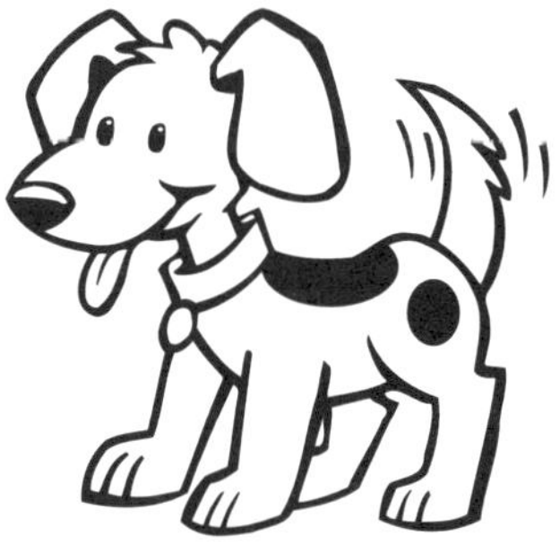

Name	Date	Helper

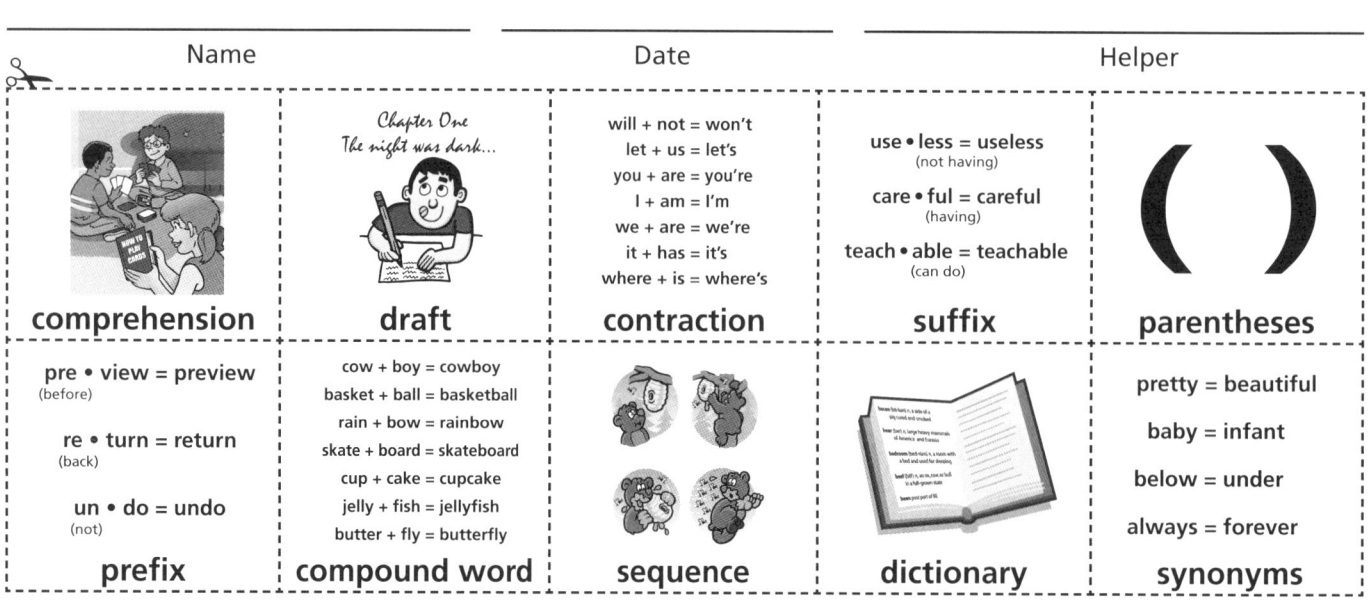

Language Arts – Say It, Paste It - Final

Directions: Have the student cut out the pictures at the bottom of the page. The helper names a picture aloud, then the student glues/tapes or places it on the big picture with the same *ending* sound.

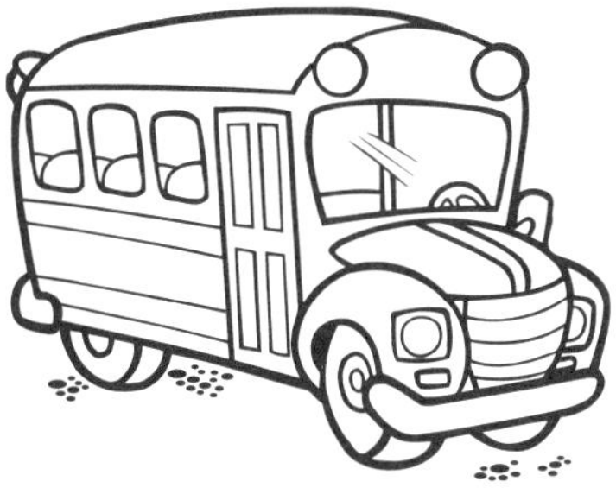

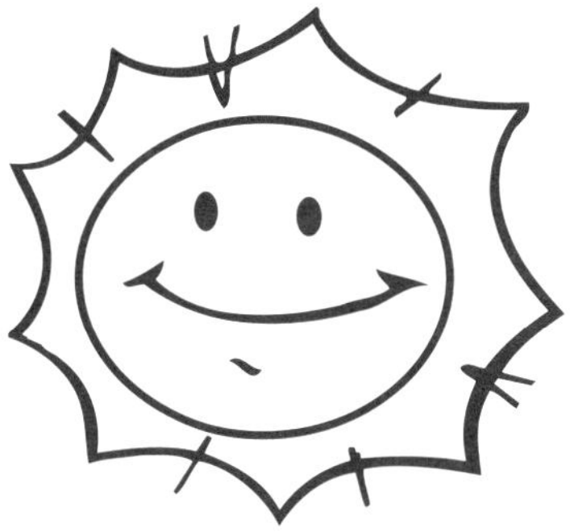

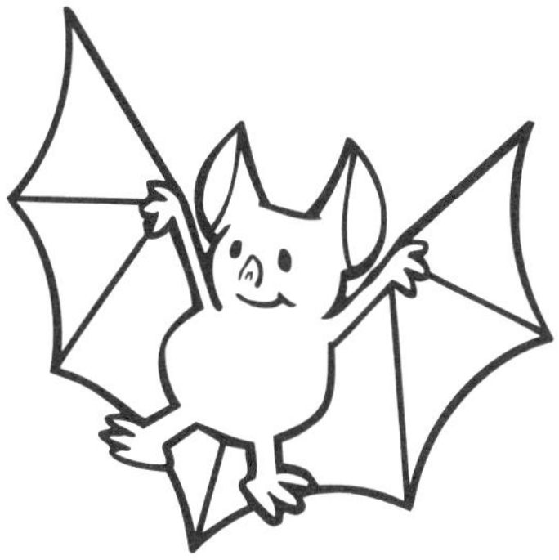

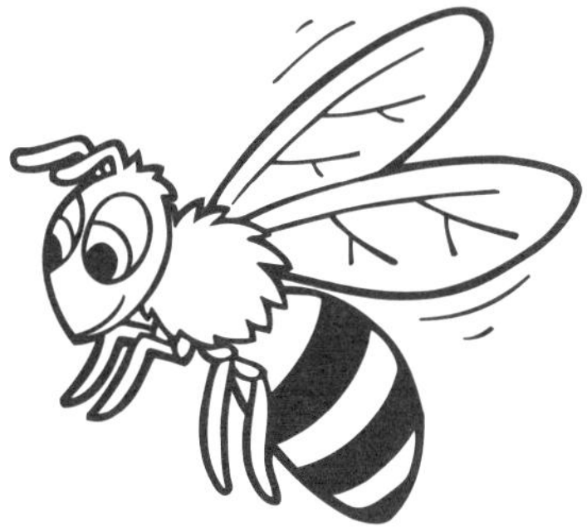

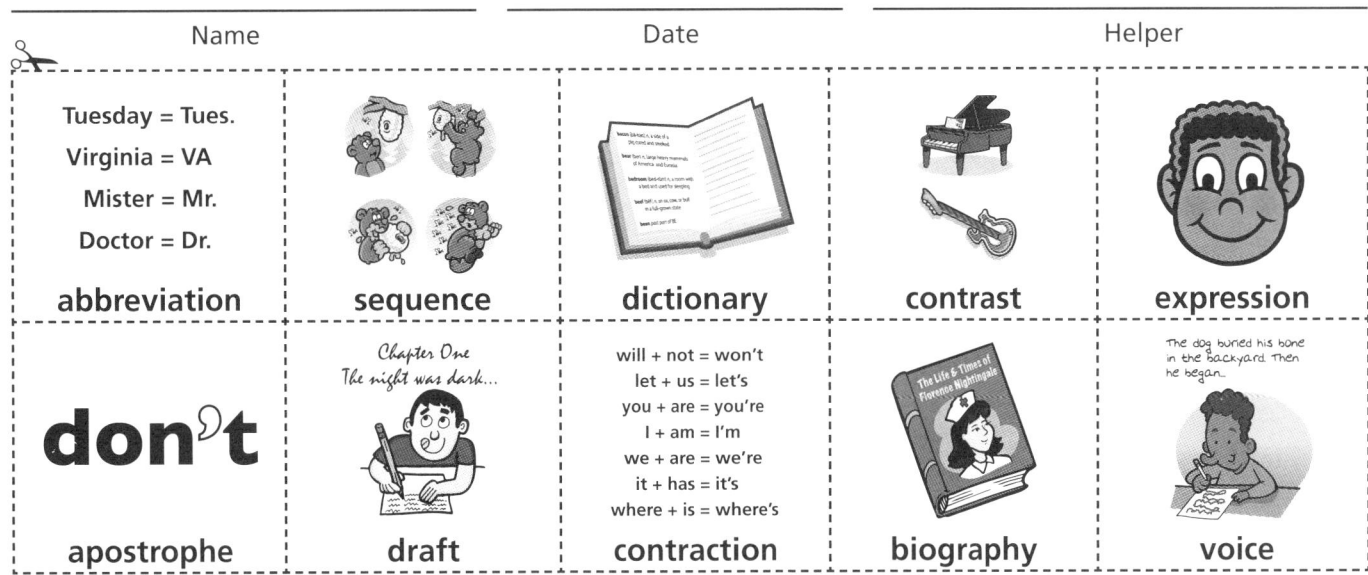

Language Arts – Breakdown

Directions: Have the students cut out the pictures. The student names each picture aloud and counts how many syllables (or parts of the word) it has. The student glues/tapes or places the picture on the side of the page with that number of syllables.

2 syllables	3 syllables

Name ____________________ Date ____________________ Helper ____________________

antonyms

contrast

the big river

adjective

use • less = useless
(not having)

care • ful = careful
(having)

teach • able = teachable
(can do)

suffix

compare

sequence

pre • view = preview
(before)

re • turn = return
(back)

un • do = undo
(not)

prefix

We went to the arcade, but it was closed.

comma

index

cow + boy = cowboy
basket + ball = basketball
rain + bow = rainbow
skate + board = skateboard
cup + cake = cupcake
jelly + fish = jellyfish
butter + fly = butterfly

compound word

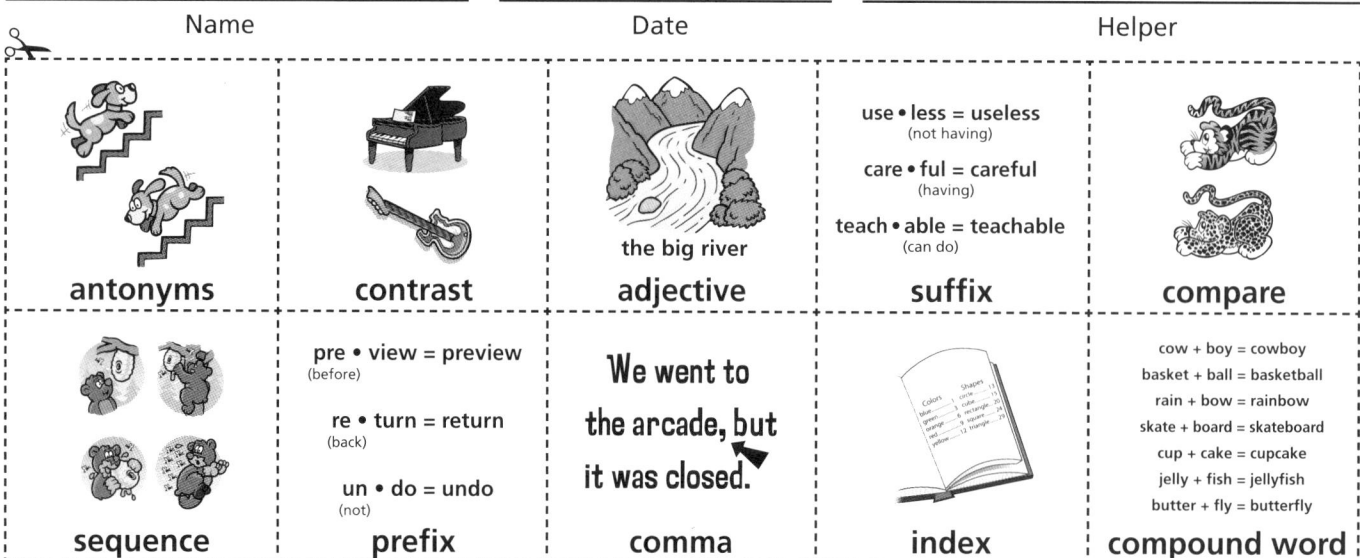

Language Arts – Syllable Search

Directions: Have the students cut out the pictures. The student names each picture aloud and counts how many syllables (or parts of the word) it has. The student glues/tapes or places the picture on the side of the page with that number of syllables. Have the student find the one word that doesn't belong and tell the number of syllables it has.

3 syllables	4 syllables

Name ____________ Date ____________ Helper ____________

pretty = beautiful baby = infant below = under always = forever **synonyms**	( ) **parentheses**	Tuesday = Tues. Virginia = VA Mister = Mr. Doctor = Dr. **abbreviation**	 **biography**	 **expression**
will + not = won't let + us = let's you + are = you're I + am = I'm we + are = we're it + has = it's where + is = where's **contraction**	 **comprehension**	" " **quotation marks**	 **dictionary**	don't **apostrophe**

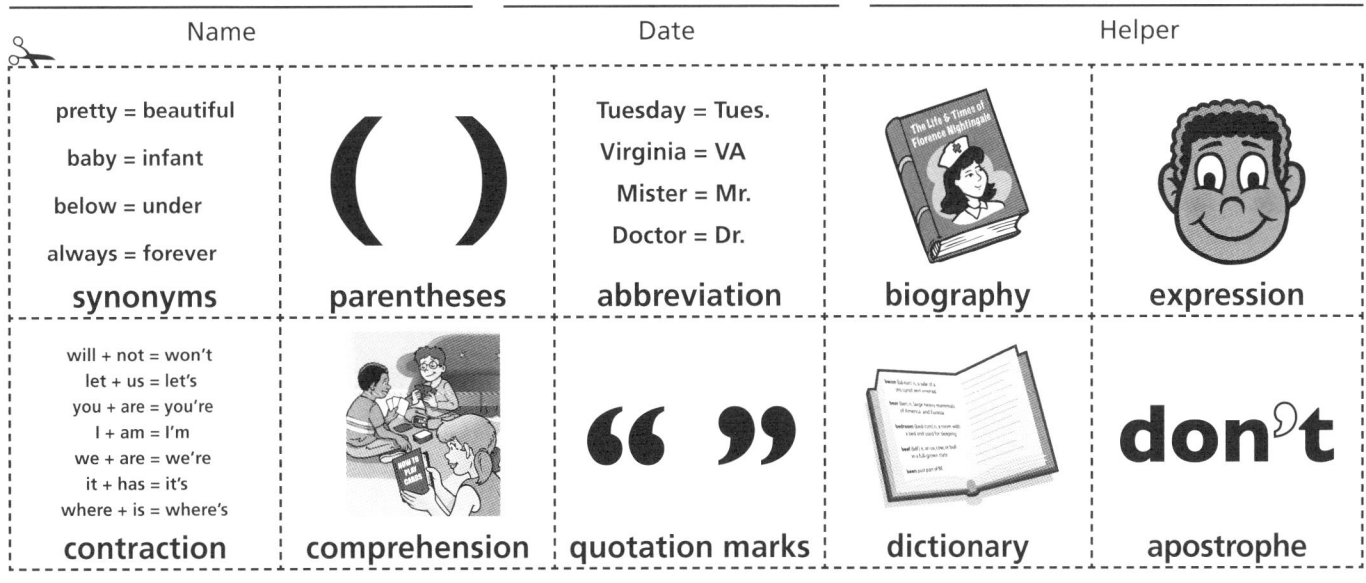

Language Arts – Word Scramble Riddle

Directions: Unscramble the words to name each picture and write the letters in the blanks. Then take the letters in the circles and write them in order in the blanks at the bottom of the page to answer the riddle.

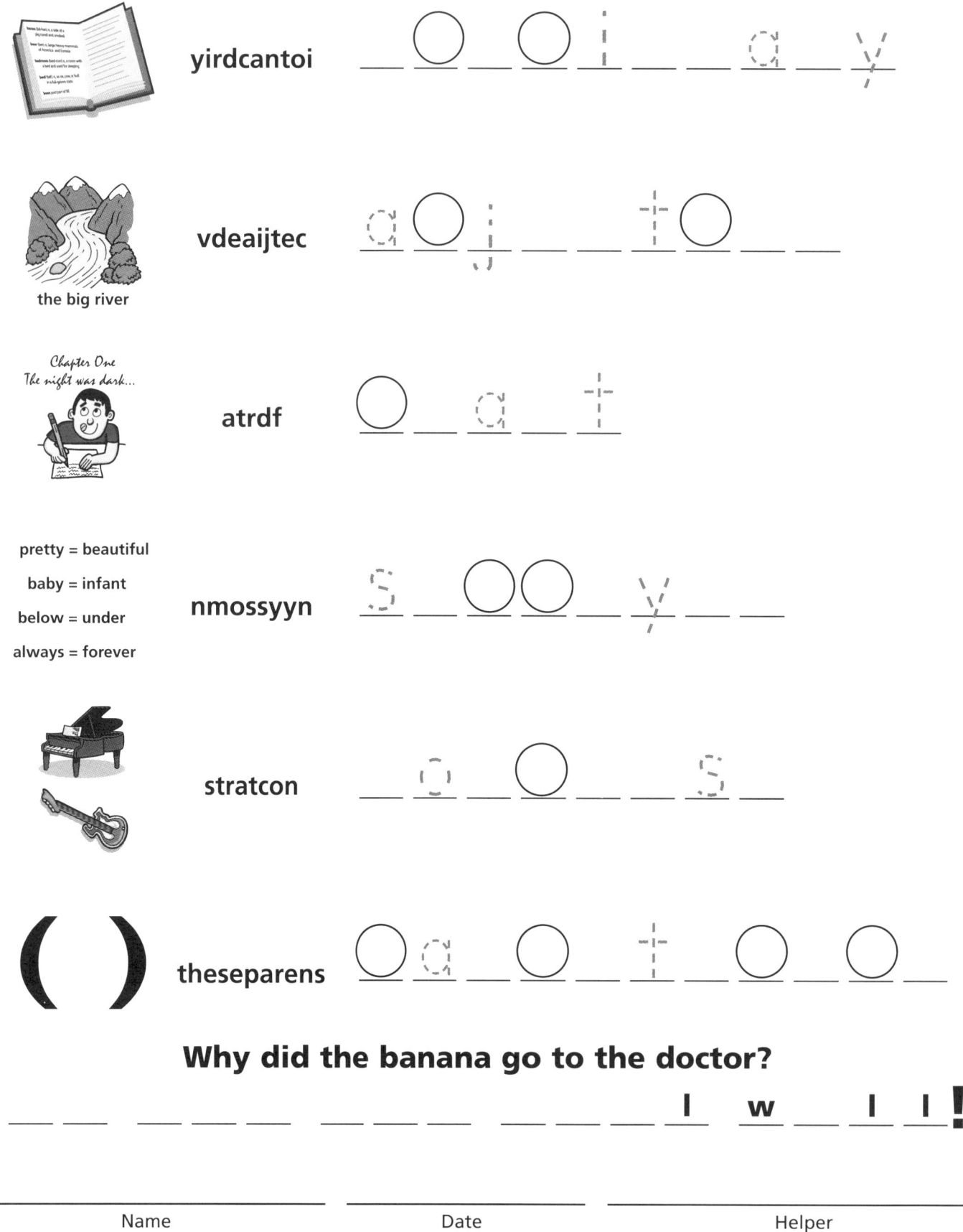

Why did the banana go to the doctor?

__ __ __ __ __ __ __ __ I w __ l l !

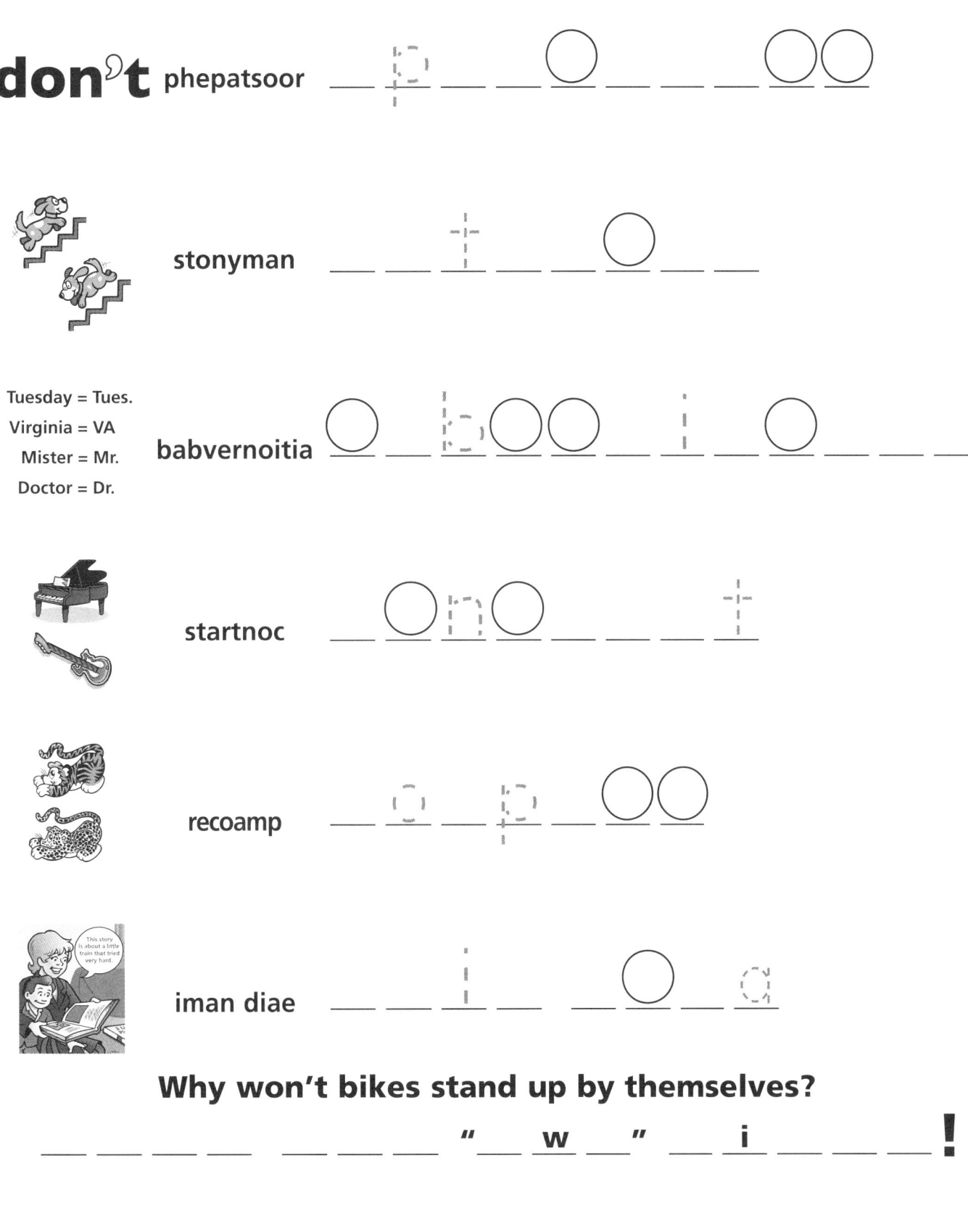

Language Arts – Word Scramble Riddle

Directions: Unscramble the words to name each picture and write the letters in the blanks. Then take the letters in the circles and write them in order in the blanks at the bottom of the page to answer the riddle.

We went to the arcade, but it was closed.

momac

henerpmocnois

" " totaqniuo skram

berv

Bill and Tom like to run.

hargpyobi

will + not = won't
let + us = let's
you + are = you're
I + am = I'm
we + are = we're
it + has = it's
where + is = where's

cottonircan

What kind of monkey can fly?

_____ _____ _____   _____ _____ _____ _____ _____   a _____ _____ _____ _____ _____ _____ _____ !

Language Arts – Writing Definitions

Directions: Read the vocabulary word below each picture. Then write a sentence beside each picture using the vocabulary word. Use the definition clues at the bottom of the page to help you.

1. **verb**

2. **draft**

3. **prefix**

   pre • view = preview (before)
   re • turn = return (back)
   un • do = undo (not)

4. **index**

5. **voice**

6. **noun**

a section in a book that lists topics and page numbers	the beginning part of a word that has its own meaning	a word for the way you express yourself in writing
a word that shows action	what you write, read over, and correct before you finish a writing project	a person, place, or thing

Name _____ Date _____ Helper _____

Language Arts – Writing Definitions

Directions: Read the vocabulary word below each picture. Then write a sentence beside each picture using the vocabulary word. Use the definition clues at the bottom of the page to help you.

1. use • less = useless
    (not having)
    care • ful = careful
    (having)
    teach • able = teachable
    (can do)

    suffix

2. **compare**

3. We went to the arcade, but it was closed.

    comma

4. will + not = won't
    let + us = let's
    you + are = you're
    I + am = I'm
    we + are = we're
    it + has = it's
    where + is = where's

    contraction

5. **dictionary**

6. **biography**

an ending part of a word that has its own meaning	a book that spells and defines many words	a mark that shows a pause in a sentence
a word that combines two words into one by using an apostrophe	a story about a person's life	finding the similarities between things

Name _____ Date _____ Helper _____

Language Arts – Writing Definitions

Directions: Read the vocabulary word below each picture. Then write a sentence beside each picture using the vocabulary word. Use the definition clues at the bottom of the page to help you.

1. **" "**
   quotation marks

2. comprehension

3. sequence

4. **don't**
   apostrophe

5. cow + boy = cowboy
   basket + ball = basketball
   rain + bow = rainbow
   skate + board = skateboard
   cup + cake = cupcake
   jelly + fish = jellyfish
   butter + fly = butterfly
   compound word

6. Tuesday = Tues.
   Virginia = VA
   Mister = Mr.
   Doctor = Dr.
   abbreviation

a mark that shows ownership or that two words have been combined into one	the order of events in a story	marks that tell when a person is speaking
a shorter version of one or more words	understanding what you read or hear	the combination of two words into one

Name   Date   Helper

Language Arts – Writing Definitions

Directions: Read the vocabulary word below each picture. Then write a sentence beside each picture using the vocabulary word. Use the definition clues at the bottom of the page to help you.

1. adjective

2. parentheses

3. antonyms

4. contrast

5. expression

6. main idea

marks used to add more information in a sentence	words that have opposite meanings	a word that describes something or someone
the way you look or speak that shows how you feel	what a story is about	finding the differences between things

Name   Date   Helper

Math – Definition Match-Up

Directions: Draw a line from the definition in Column A to the word that matches it in Column B. Read/Say the definition and its matching vocabulary word aloud.

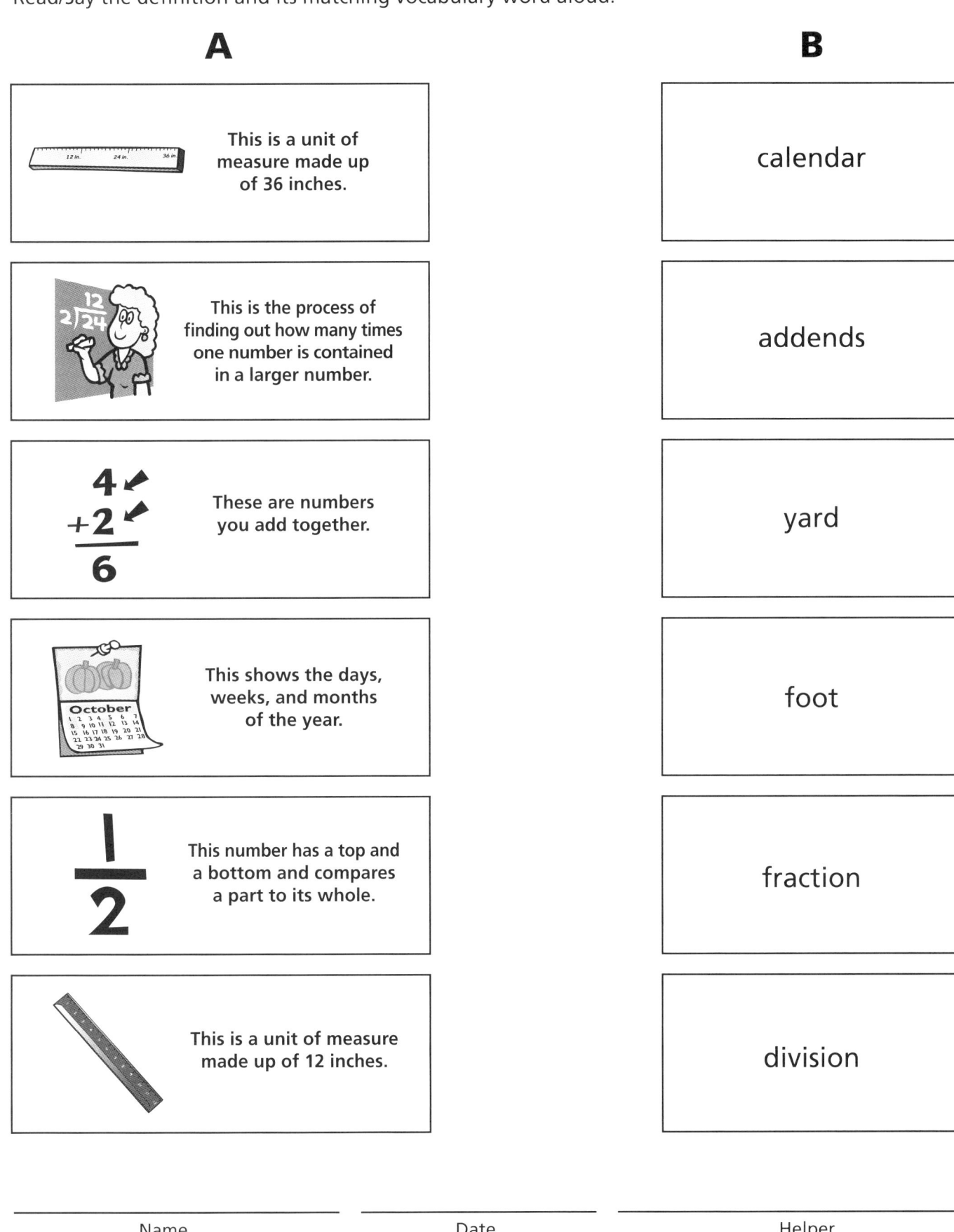

Math – Star Match-Up

Directions: Cut out the definitions at the bottom of the page. Shuffle the definitions and place them facedown. Have the students take turns reading the definitions and placing them next to the correct picture. The first player to find the star is the winner.

dime

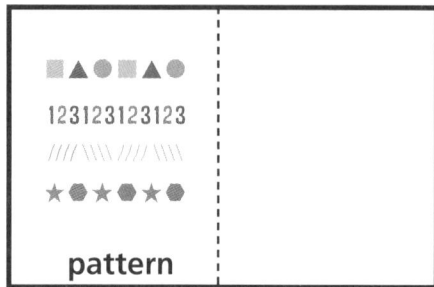
pattern

estimate

picture graph

data

analog clock

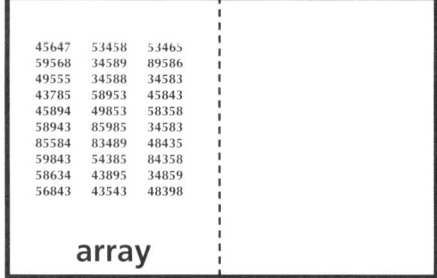
array

digital clock

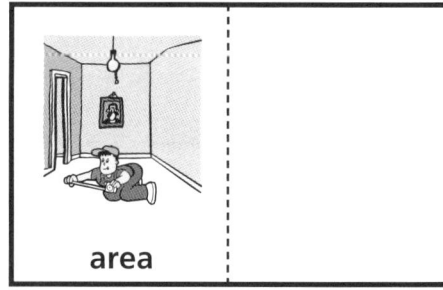
area

This object shows the time using numbers and hour and minute hands.	This object shows the time electronically with numbers.	This is when you guess what a number or amount will be.	This is a collection of measurements, values, or facts used to make calculations.	This is a coin that is worth ten cents.
	This is a diagram or chart that shows information using images.	This is the measure of the surface of an object.	This is an orderly arrangement of information in rows and columns.	This is a collection of lines, shapes, or numbers that repeat over and over.

Name _____ Date _____ Helper _____

28

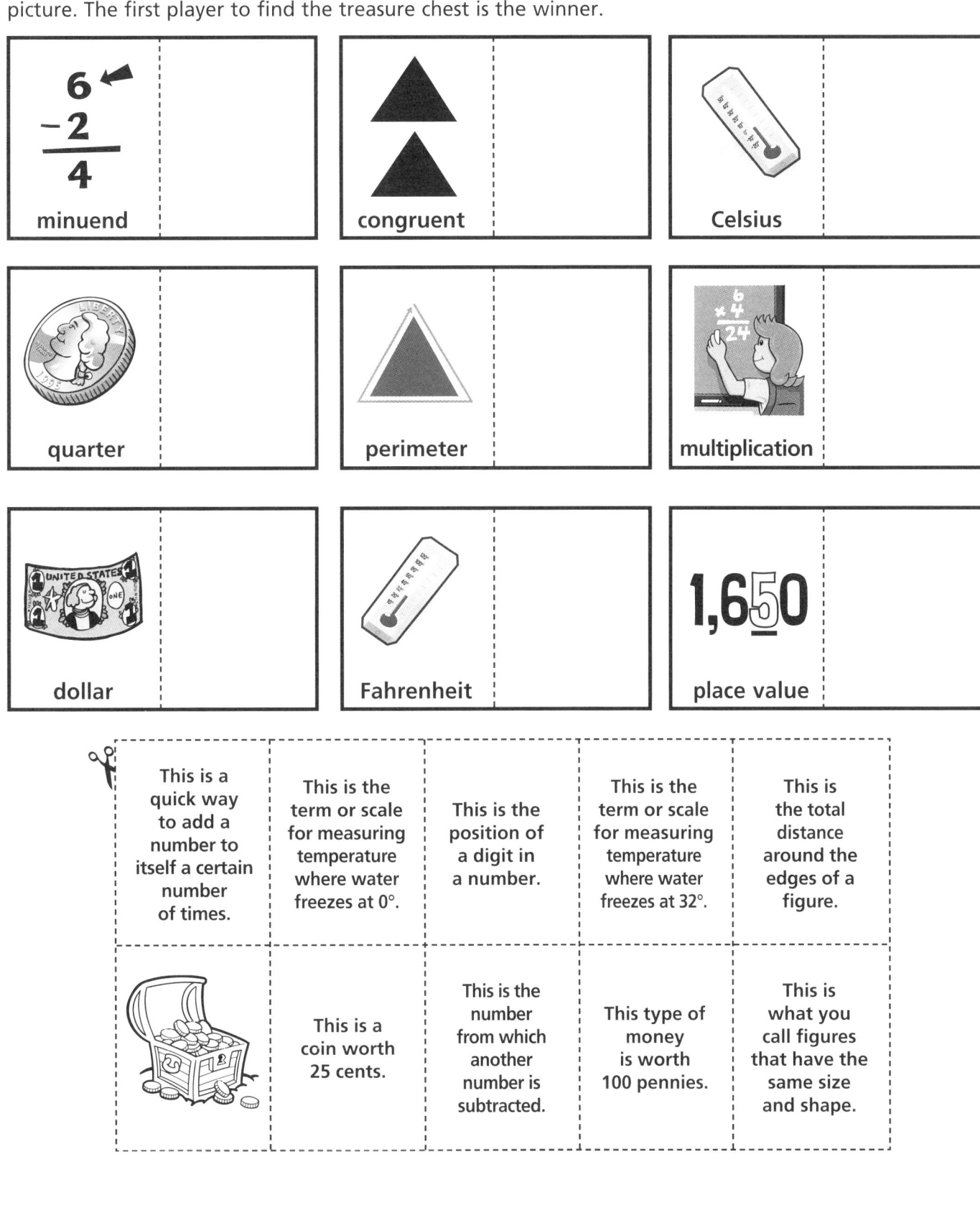

Math – What's the Correct Meaning?

Directions: Read each sentence. Circle the picture and definition on the right that have the correct meaning for the word in bold.

1. The **volume** of my shoe box is 300 cubic inches.

    This is the amount of space an object takes up.

    This is a unit of measure made up of 12 inches.

2. Please mark the date for the party on your **calendar**.

    This shows the days, weeks, and months of the year.

    This is a collection of lines, shapes, or numbers that repeat over and over.

3. The **addends** 12 and 8 will total 20.

    This is the process of finding out how many times one number is contained in a larger number.

   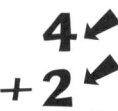 These are numbers you add together.

4. The rug measures one **yard** on each side.

    This number has a top and a bottom and compares a part to its whole.

    This is a unit of measure made up of 36 inches.

5. I need one more **foot** of ribbon to make a bow.

    This is a unit of measure made up of 12 inches.

    This is the measure of the surface of an object.

6. Grandpa ate only a **fraction** of his hamburger.

    This is when you guess what a number or amount will be.

   This number has a top and a bottom and compares a part to its whole.

_____   _____   _____
Name   Date   Helper

Math – What's the Correct Meaning?

Directions: Read each sentence. Circle the picture and definition on the right that have the correct meaning for the word in bold.

1. The **division** of students from the entire school gave us 38 teams of 4.

   This is a quick way to add a number to itself a certain number of times.

   This is the process of finding out how many times one number is contained in a larger number.

2. I need one more **dime** to buy some chips.

   This is a coin that is worth ten cents.

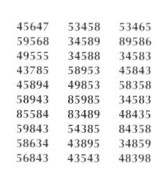

   This is an orderly arrangement of information in rows and columns.

3. Please repeat the same **pattern** of blue, white, and red.

   This is a collection of measurements, values, or facts used to make calculations.

   This is a collection of lines, shapes, or numbers that repeat over and over.

4. Each student must **estimate** how much money he or she needs for the field trip.

   This is the measure of the surface of an object.

   This is when you guess what a number or amount will be.

5. The **picture graph** shows the fourth grade outsold the other grades during the candy sale.

   This is a diagram or chart that shows information using images.

   This is what you call figures that have the same size and shape.

6. The **data** proves that we need to hire more employees.

   This type of money is worth 100 pennies.

   This is a collection of measurements, values, or facts used to make calculations.

_____ _____ _____
Name   Date   Helper

Math – What's the Correct Meaning?

Directions: Read each sentence. Circle the picture and definition on the right that have the correct meaning for the word in bold.

1. The hands on the **analog clock** read 6:15.

   This object shows the time electronically with numbers.

   This object shows the time using numbers and hour and minute hands.

2. The **array** of information shows that student grades are improving each month.

   This is an orderly arrangement of information in rows and columns.

   This shows the days, weeks, and months of the year.

3. The **digital clock** kept blinking "12:00" after the power went out.

   This object shows the time electronically with numbers.

   This is the term or scale for measuring temperature where water freezes at 0°.

4. How much carpet do we need to cover the **area** of the basement floor.

   This is the measure of the surface of an object.

   This is the amount of space an object takes up.

5. Subtracting 12 cans from a **minuend** of 22 leaves 10 cans.

   This is the process of finding out how many times one number is contained in a larger number.

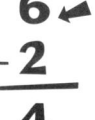

   This is the number from which another number is subtracted.

6. Do you have a **quarter** for these 25 pennies?

   This type of money is worth 100 pennies.

   This is a coin worth 25 cents.

_____   _____   _____
Name   Date   Helper

Math – Answer It!

Directions: Read each question. Then put an X on the letter next to the picture and vocabulary word that best answers the question.

1. Which piece of money equals 100 pennies?

    A) dollar   B) quarter

2. Which word means "equal in size and shape"?

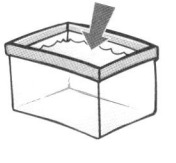

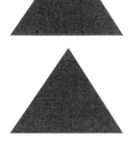

    A) volume   B) congruent

3. Which is the measure of the distance around the fence outside?

    A) division   B) perimeter

4. Which scale measures temperature of freezing water at 32°?

    A) Fahrenheit   B) Celsius

5. Which is a quick way to add the same number many times?

    A) division   B) multiplication

6. Which tells the position of a digit in a number?

    A) fraction   B) place value

Name _____   Date _____   Helper _____

Math – Answer It!

Directions: Read each question. Then put an X on the letter next to the picture and vocabulary word that best answers the question.

1. Which scale measures freezing water at 0°?

    A)  Fahrenheit   B)  Celsius

2. What gives the measurement of how much water a bathtub can hold?

    A)  volume   B)  perimeter

3. What do you use to find today's date?

    A)  calendar   B)  data

4. What are numbers that you add together?

    A) minuend   B) addends

5. What is a measurement of 36 inches?

    A)  foot   B)  yard

6. Which has more value?

    A)  dime   B)  quarter

Name _____ Date _____ Helper _____

Math – Answer It!

Directions: Read each question. Then put an X on the letter next to the picture and vocabulary word that best answers the question.

1. What repeats itself over and over again? A) fraction   B) pattern

2. Which means "to make a good guess"? A) estimate   B) array

3. What uses images to display information? A) calendar   B) picture graph

4. What is a collection of all types of information? A) data   B) area

5. Which clock uses hands to tell time? A) digital   B) analog

6. What is an arrangement of information in rows and column? A) picture graph   B) array

_____   _____   _____
Name   Date   Helper

Math – Sentence Completion

Directions: Read each sentence below. Complete each sentence using a vocabulary word from the Word/Picture Bank. Write the word in the blank.

Word/Picture Bank

digital clock	area	minuend	quarter	dollar
congruent	perimeter	Fahrenheit	multiplication	place value

1. A _____ has a value of one hundred cents.

2. Farmer Dan needs 1,000 feet of fence to outline the _____ of his pasture.

3. The _____ of the 7 in 2,174 is the tens place.

4. Water boils at 212° and freezes at 32° _____ .

5. Subtracting 30 from a _____ of 62 leaves a difference of 32.

6. The rug is not large enough to cover the _____ of this room.

7. Telling time on a _____ is easier than reading the hands of an analog clock.

8. I need one more _____ for the gumball machine.

9. _____ is the easiest way to add one number many times.

10. Two figures that are alike in every way are _____ .

_____ _____ _____
Name   Date   Helper

Math – Sentence Completion

Directions: Read each sentence below. Complete each sentence using a vocabulary word from the Word/Picture Bank. Write the word in the blank.

Word/Picture Bank

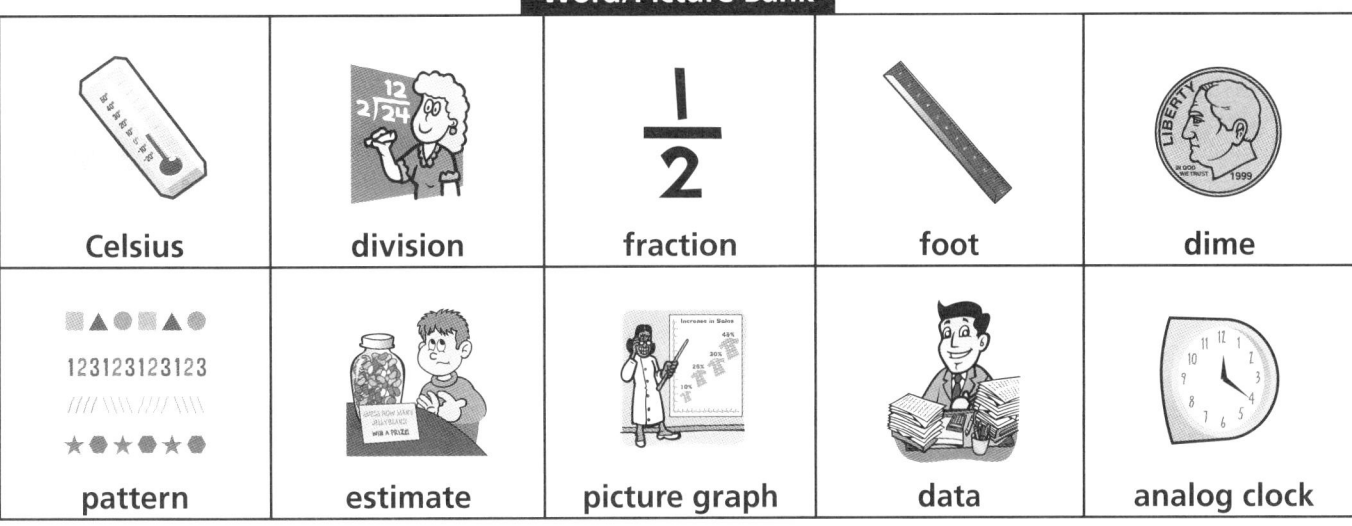

Celsius	division	fraction	foot	dime
pattern	estimate	picture graph	data	analog clock

1. Water freezes at 0° _____ .

2. The hands of the _____ read 3:17.

3. Does anyone have a _____ for a nickel and five pennies?

4. The collection of _____ proves that our candy sales have improved over last year's sales.

5. For our project, we made a _____ using drawings of cupcakes to compare how many cupcakes each class sold.

6. We threaded beads onto a necklace using a _____ of two red, two blue, and three white beads.

7. After the _____ of students, there were 10 groups of 13 students.

8. Knowing how many guests are attending the party will give us an _____ of how much food to prepare.

9. The judges were allowed to taste only a _____ of the whole pie for the contest.

10. I needed an extra _____ of rope to tie the boat to the dock.

_____   _____   _____
Name   Date   Helper

Math – Sentence Completion

Directions: Read each sentence below. Complete each sentence using a vocabulary word from the Word/Picture Bank. Write the word in the blank.

Word/Picture Bank

volume	calendar	addends	yard	array
area	minuend	congruent	perimeter	estimate

1. The teacher wants us to _____ the number of candies in the jar.

2. We have enough carpet to cover an _____ of 500 square feet.

3. Each _____ of ribbon for our project must measure exactly 36 inches.

4. The _____ of information helped us figure out which items sold best in different months of the year.

5. The _____ of our swimming pool is much larger than our neighbors' pool.

6. Please mark the date of your dentist appointment on your _____ .

7. The numbers 17 and 26 are _____ of 43.

8. If you subtract 37 from a _____ of 100, your answer will be 63.

9. What is the distance around the _____ of your yard?

10. A triangle and a square can never be _____.

_____   _____   _____
Name   Date   Helper

Math – Which Ones Belong Together?

Directions: Cut out the three pictures in Row 1. Glue the two pictures that go together in the empty boxes on the left. Tell why the two pictures go together. Complete the page one row at a time.

1.

| 1. | array | calendar | data |

2. | dime | quarter | picture graph |

3. | minuend | multiplication | division |

4. | yard | volume | foot |

5. | minuend | addends | estimate |

6. | Celsius | foot | Fahrenheit |

Name   Date   Helper

Math – Which Doesn't Belong?

Directions: Read/Listen carefully to each group of words. Mark an X through the word that doesn't belong. Tell how the other words relate to each other.

1. foot, yard, perimeter, calendar

2. quarter, estimate, dollar, dime

3. data, array, picture graph, yard

4. area, volume, perimeter, Celsius

5. analog clock, perimeter, digital clock, calendar

6. division, multiplication, minuend, Fahrenheit

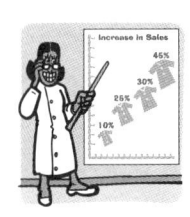

7. multiplication, addends, place value, foot

8. foot, perimeter, yard, dollar

9. minuend, fraction, addend, estimate

10. pattern, data, dime, array

_____   _____   _____
Name   Date   Helper

Math – Which Doesn't Belong?

Directions: Put an X through the picture in each row that doesn't belong. Tell why the other two pictures belong together.

1. dime | yard | dollar

2. estimate | picture graph | data

3. area | congruent | perimeter

4. Fahrenheit | foot | Celsius

5. calendar | analog clock | pattern

6. minuend | addends | area

Math – Say It, Paste It - Initial

Directions: Have the student cut out the pictures at the bottom of the page. The helper names a picture aloud, then the student glues/tapes or places it on the big picture with the same *beginning* sound.

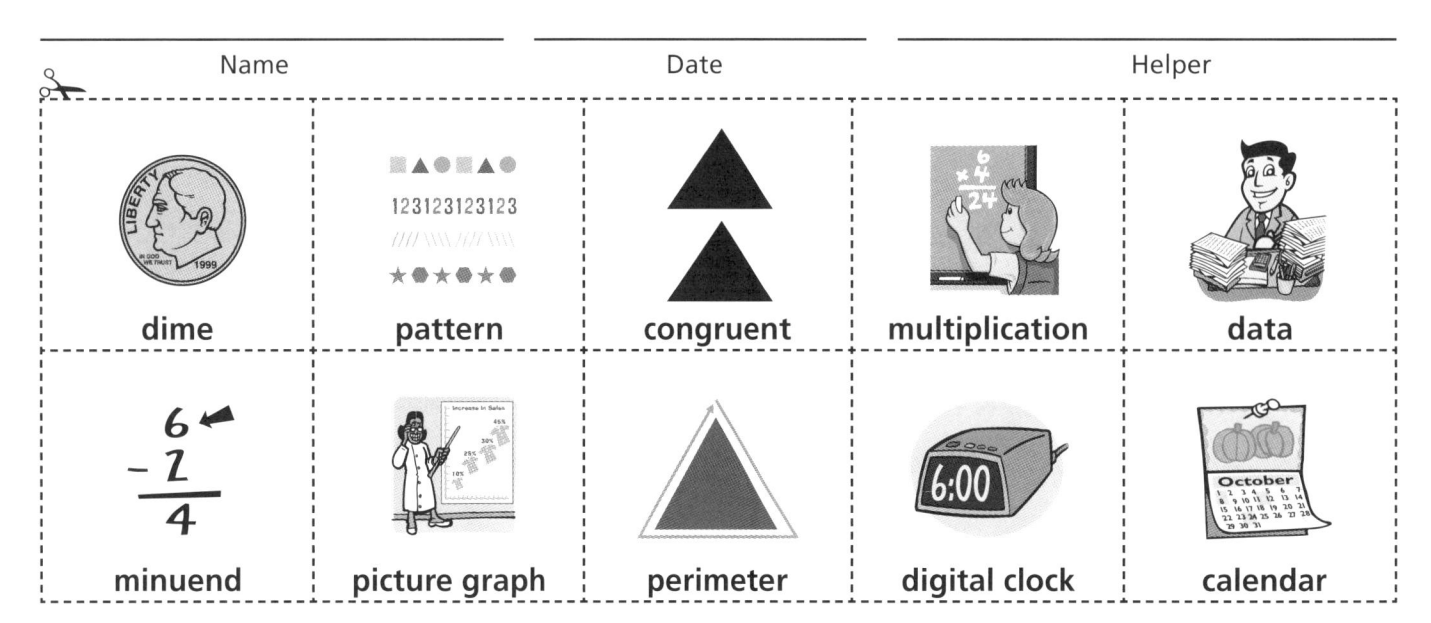

_____ _____ _____
Name   Date   Helper

| dime | pattern | congruent | multiplication | data |
| minuend | picture graph | perimeter | digital clock | calendar |

42

Math – Say It, Paste It - Final

Directions: Have the student cut out the pictures at the bottom of the page. The helper names a picture aloud, then the student glues/tapes or places it on the big picture with the same *ending* sound.

Name	Date	Helper

| Fahrenheit | estimate | dime | yard | pattern |
| division | congruent | minuend | fraction | volume |

Math – Breakdown

Directions: Have the students cut out the pictures. The student names each picture aloud and counts how many syllables (or parts of the word) it has. The student glues/tapes or places the picture on the side of the page with that number of syllables.

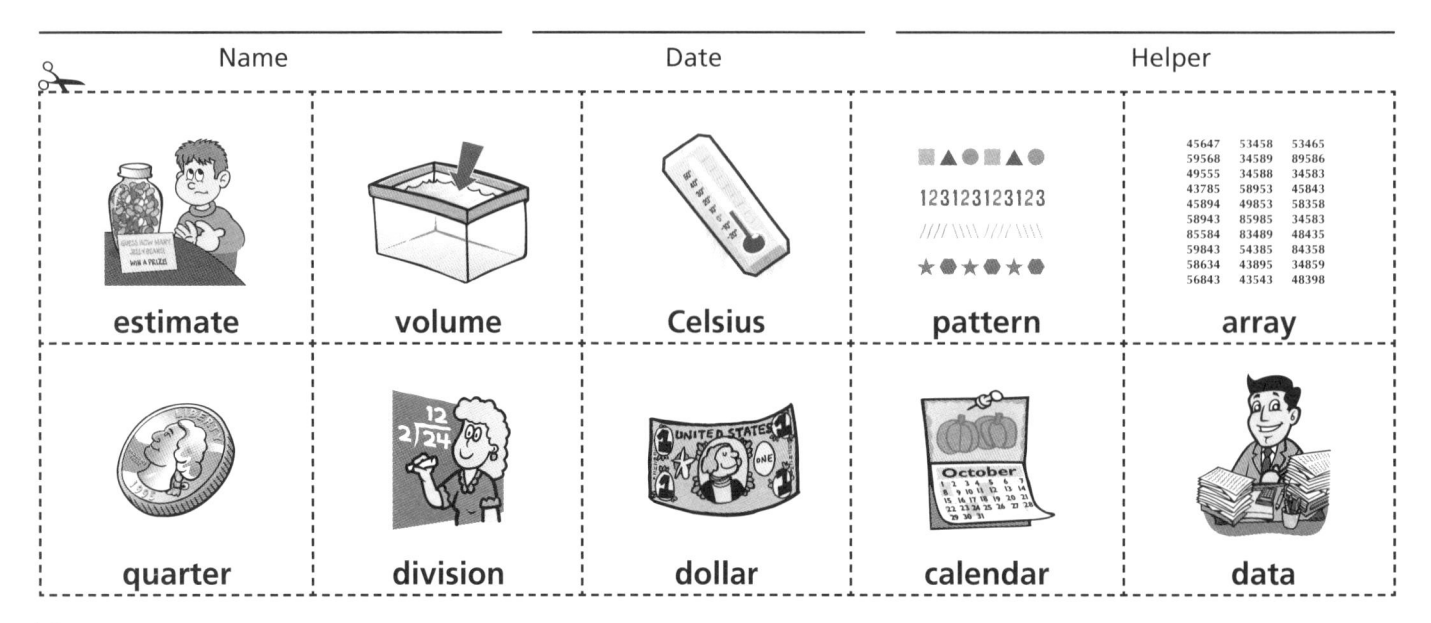

2 syllables	3 syllables

_____ _____ _____
Name Date Helper

estimate	volume	Celsius	pattern	array
quarter	division	dollar	calendar	data

Math – Syllable Search

Directions: Have the students cut out the pictures. The student names each picture aloud and counts how many syllables (or parts of the word) it has. The student glues/tapes or places the picture on the side of the page with that number of syllables. Have the students find the one word that doesn't belong and tell the number of syllables it has.

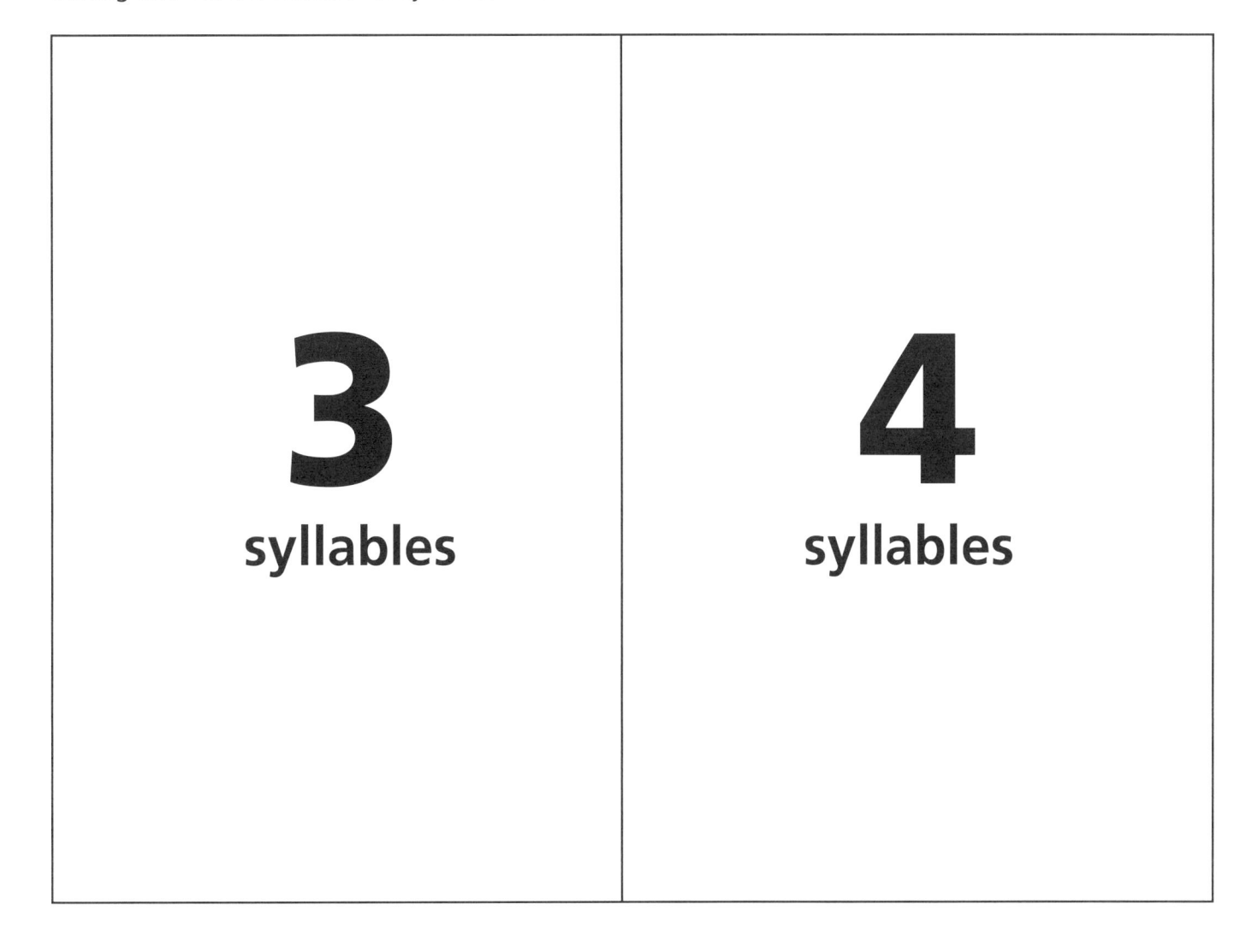

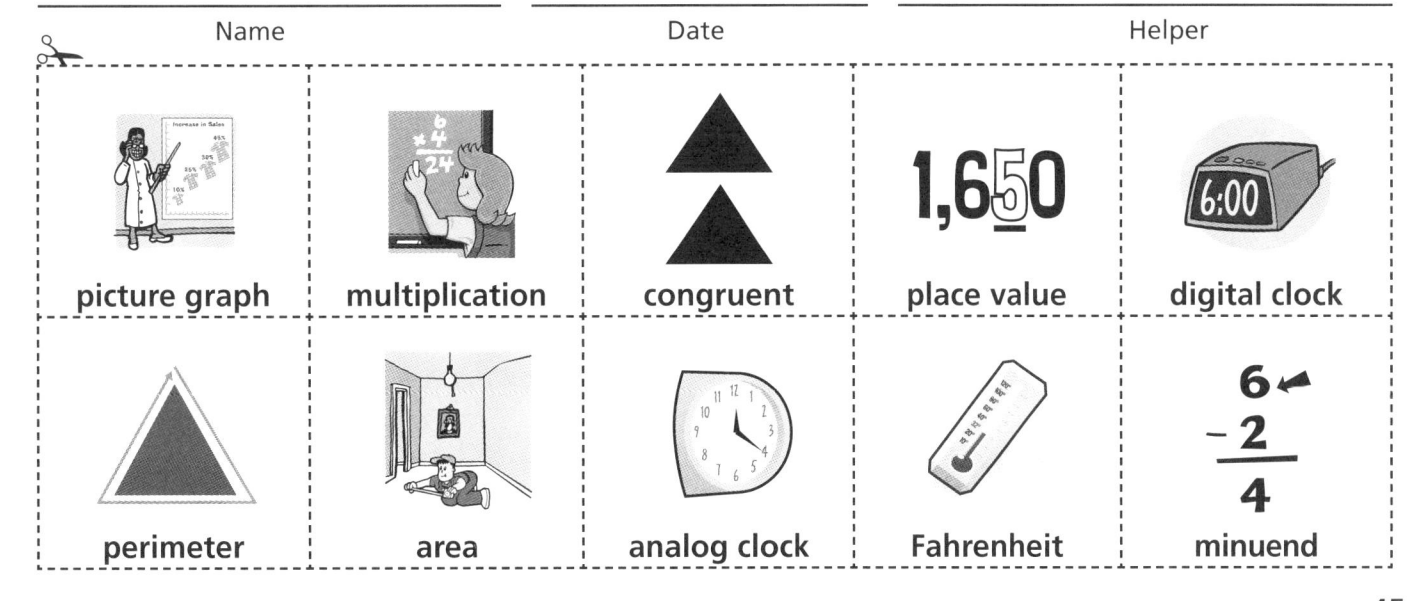

3 syllables

4 syllables

Name	Date	Helper

picture graph	multiplication	congruent	place value	digital clock
perimeter	area	analog clock	Fahrenheit	minuend

Math – Word Scramble Riddle

Directions: Unscramble the words to name each picture and write the letters in the blanks. Then take the letters in the circles and write them in order in the blanks at the bottom of the page to answer the riddle.

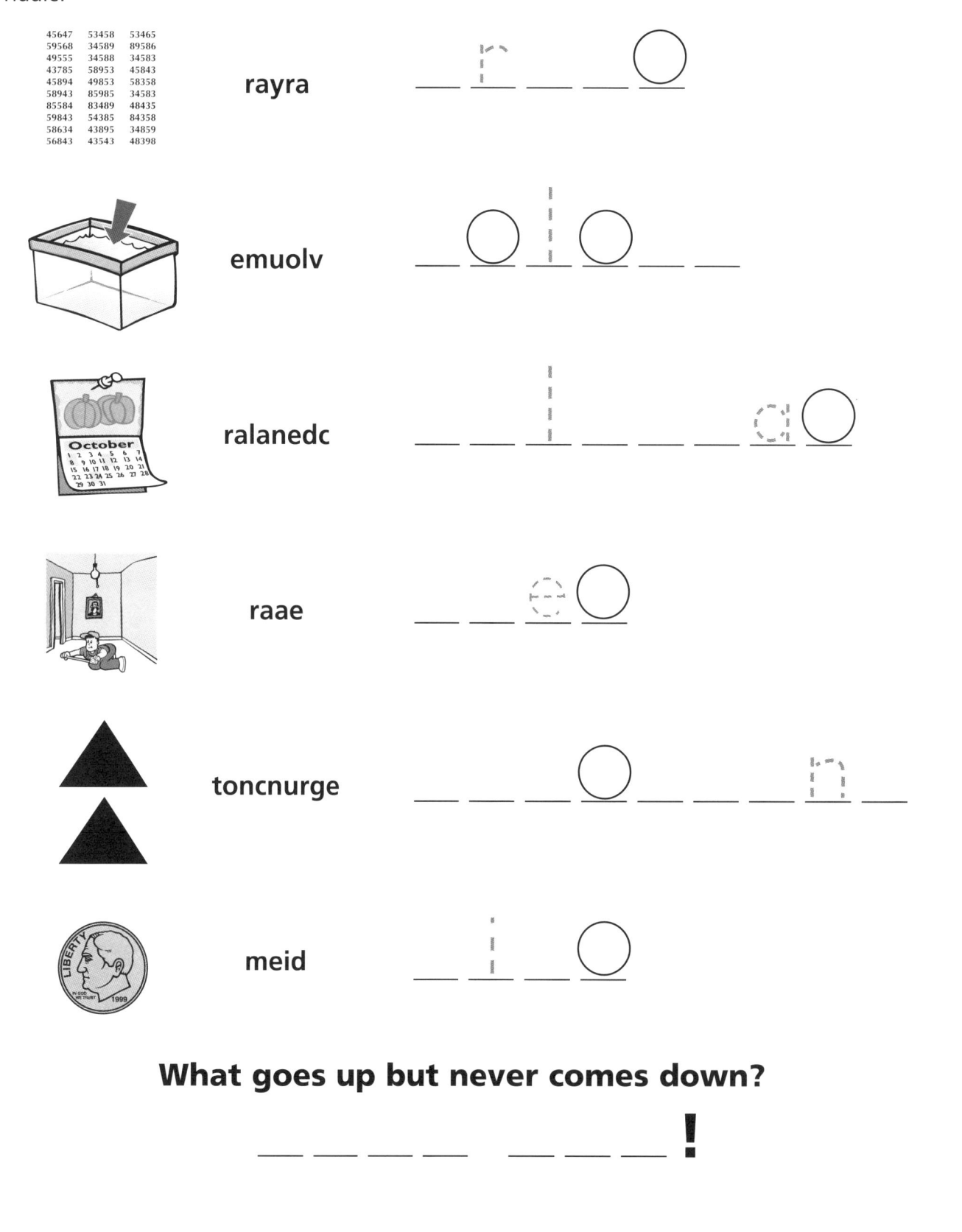

rayra _ r _ _ ◯

emuolv ◯ _ l _ ◯ _ _

ralanedc _ _ _ i _ _ d ◯

raae _ _ e ◯

toncnurge _ _ _ ◯ _ _ _ n _

meid _ i _ ◯

What goes up but never comes down?

_ _ _ _ _ _ !

Name Date Helper

46

Math – Word Scramble Riddle

Directions: Unscramble the words to name each picture and write the letters in the blanks. Then take the letters in the circles and write them in order in the blanks at the bottom of the page to answer the riddle.

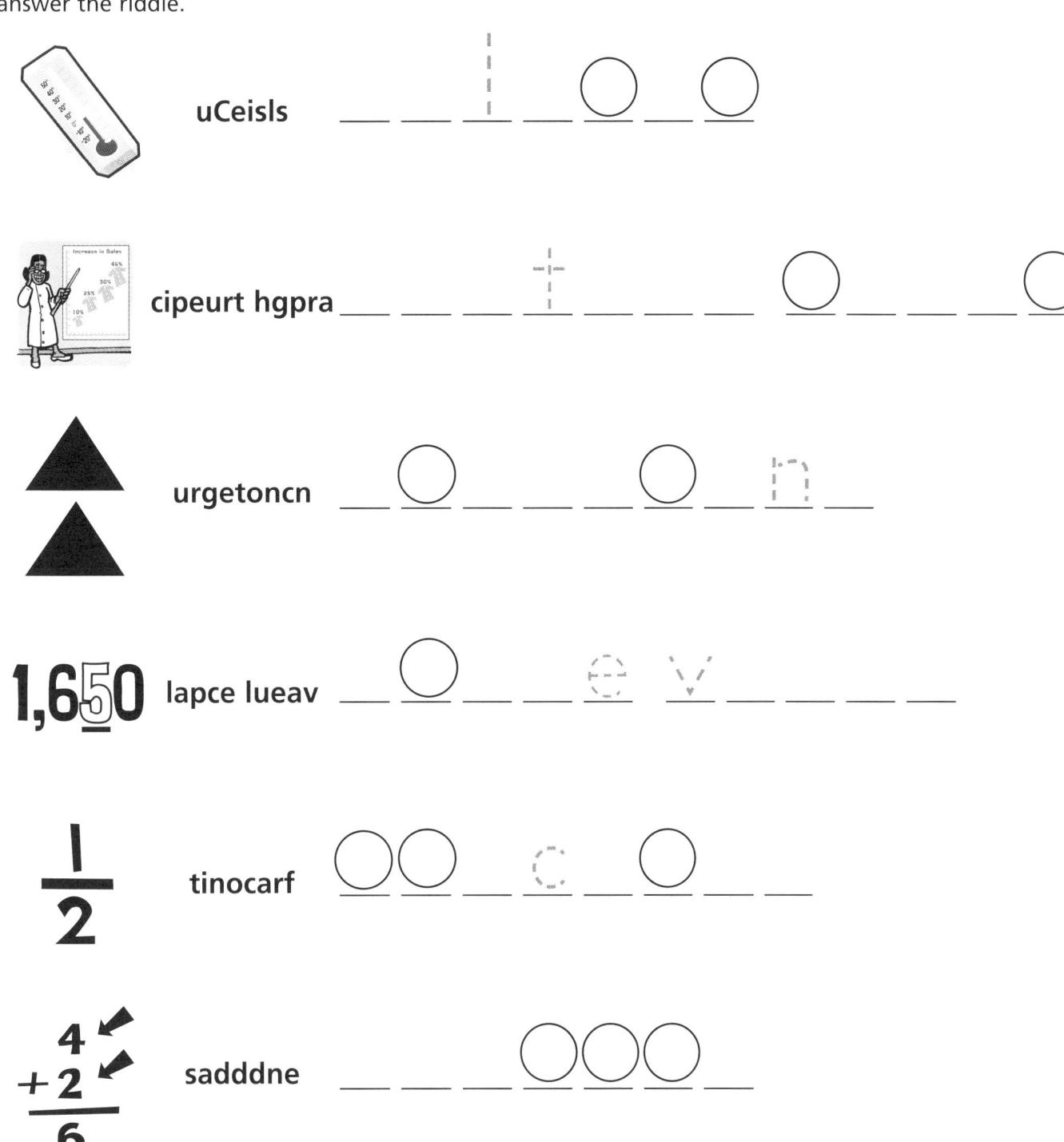

uCeisls __ __ i ◯ ◯ __

cipeurt hgpra __ __ __ __ t __ __ ◯ __ __ __ ◯

urgetoncn ◯ __ __ ◯ __ __ n __

lapce lueav ◯ __ __ e v __ __ __

tinocarf ◯◯ __ c __ ◯ __

sadddne __ __ __ ◯◯◯ __

Who did Frankenstein take to the school dance?

H __ __ " __ __ __ __ __ __ " __ __ __ __ __ __ __ !

Math – Word Scramble Riddle

Directions: Unscramble the words to name each picture and write the letters in the blanks. Then take the letters in the circles and write them in order in the blanks at the bottom of the page to answer the riddle.

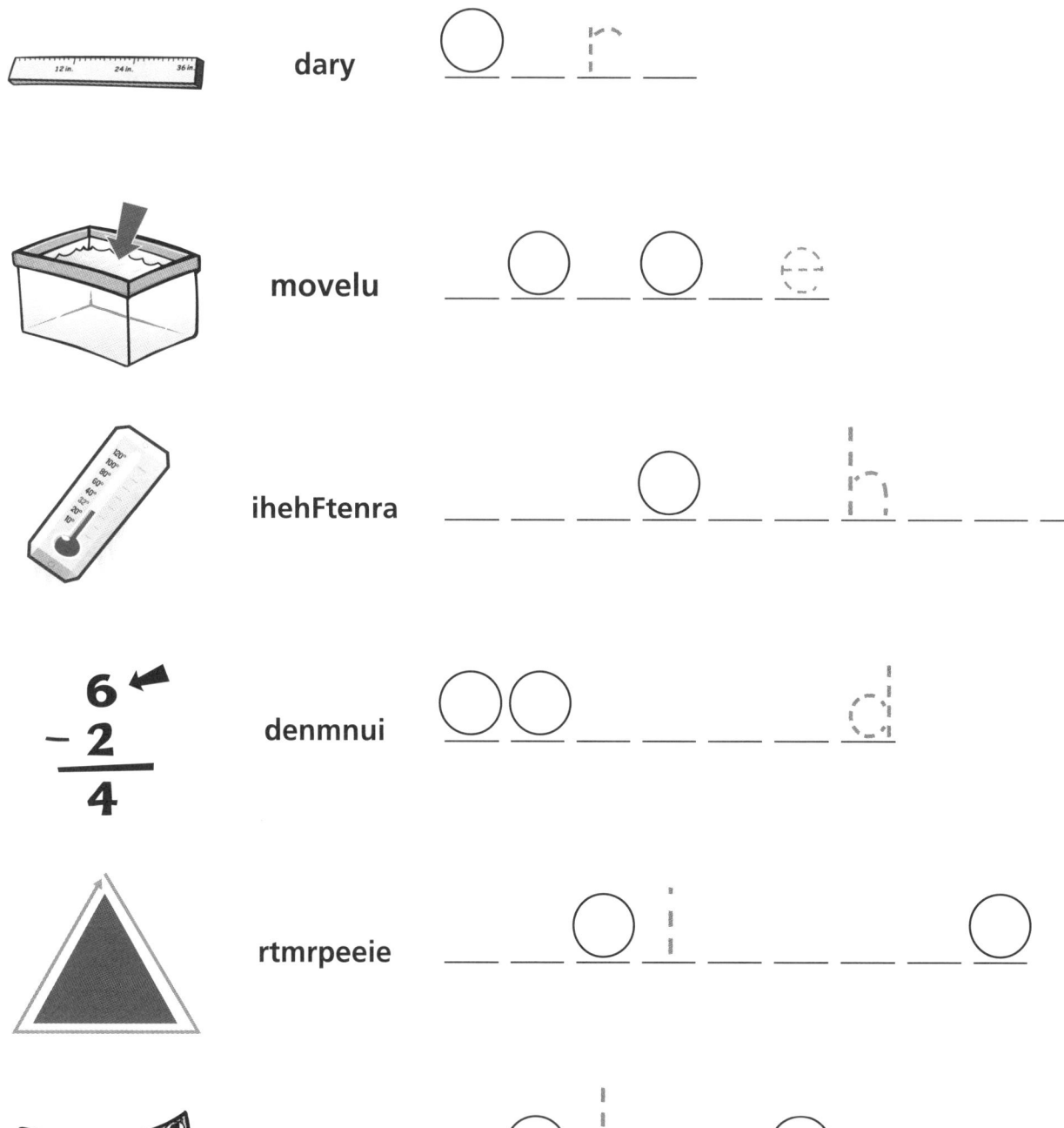

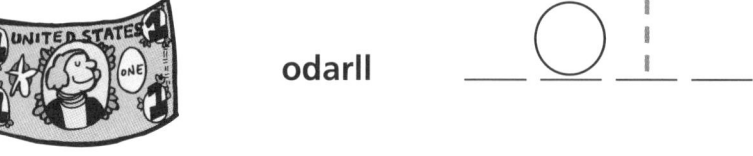

dary   _○_ _ _r_ _

movelu   _ _○_ _○_ _e_

ihehFtenra   _ _ _○_ _ _h_ _ _ _

denmnui   _○○_ _ _ _ _d_

rtmrpeeie _ _○_i_ _ _ _ _○_

odarll   _ _○_i_ _○_

What turns everything around but does not move?

___ ___ ___   ___ ___ ___ ___ ___ ___!

Math – Writing Definitions

Directions: Read the vocabulary word below each picture. Then write a sentence beside each picture using the vocabulary word. Use the definition clues at the bottom of the page to help you.

1. array

2. calendar

3. area

4. congruent

5. picture graph

6. Celsius

a chart that shows information using images	shows the days, weeks, and months of the year	the measure of an object's surface
the scale for measuring temperature where water freezes at 0°	figures that have the same size and shape	an arrangement of information in rows and columns

Name Date Helper

Math – Writing Definitions

Directions: Read the vocabulary word below each picture. Then write a sentence beside each picture using the vocabulary word. Use the definition clues at the bottom of the page to help you.

1. estimate

2. addends

3. fraction

4. quarter

5. dime

6. data

guessing a number or amount	a coin that is worth ten cents	numbers to be added together
a part to a whole	a collection of measurements, values, or facts	a coin worth 25 cents

_____   _____   _____
Name   Date   Helper

Math – Writing Definitions

Directions: Read the vocabulary word below each picture. Then write a sentence beside each picture using the vocabulary word. Use the definition clues at the bottom of the page to help you.

1. foot

2. pattern

3. digital clock

4. multiplication

5. analog clock

6. division

shows the time using numbers and hour and minute hands	a measure of 12 inches	shapes or numbers that repeat over and over
a quick way to add a number many times	finding out how many times one number is contained in a larger number	shows the time electronically with numbers

Name _____ Date _____ Helper _____

Math – Writing Definitions

Directions: Read the vocabulary words below each picture. Then write a sentence beside each picture using the vocabulary word. Use the definition clues at the bottom of the page to help you.

1. **1,6_5_0**
   place value

2. **dollar**

3. **perimeter**

4. **yard**

5. **volume**

6. **Fahrenheit**

measuring temperature where water freezes at 32°	a measurement of 36 inches	how much space an object takes up
the distance around the edges of a figure	paper bill equal to 100 cents	the position of a digit in a number

_____   _____   _____
Name   Date   Helper

Science – Definition Match-Up

Directions: Draw a line from the definition in Column A to the word that matches it in Column B. Read/Say the definition and its matching vocabulary word aloud.

A

This is the process of a liquid changing into a gas.

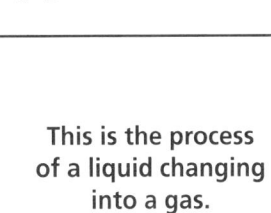

These are the smallest parts of living things.

This means to study something closely to learn facts or information about it.

This is the name for a living plant or animal.

This is the process of a gas changing into a liquid.

This is water, rain, snow, or hail falling from the sky.

B

precipitation

evaporation

condensation

organism

investigate

cells

Name   Date   Helper

Science – Star Match-Up

Directions: Cut out the definitions at the bottom of the page. Shuffle the definitions and place them facedown. Have the students take turns reading the definitions and placing them next to the correct pictures. The first player to find the star is the winner.

classify	recycle	atmosphere
observe	magnet	rotate
weather	cloud	motion

| This is when you sort objects or living things into groups. | This is the act of moving from one place to another. | This is the wind, temperature, rainfall, and clouds in a particular place and time. | This means to turn around and around on a center point or axis. | This is when you watch something carefully and gather information about it. |
| ★ | This is a solid object that attracts metal objects. | This is made up of the invisible gases that surround Earth. | This means to create something new from used material. | This is a collection of water or ice droplets in the sky that you can see. |

_____   _____   _____
Name   Date   Helper

Science – Treasure Chest Match-Up

Directions: Cut out the definitions at the bottom of the page. Shuffle the definitions and place them facedown. Have the students take turns reading the definitions and placing them next to the correct pictures. The first player to find the treasure chest is the winner.

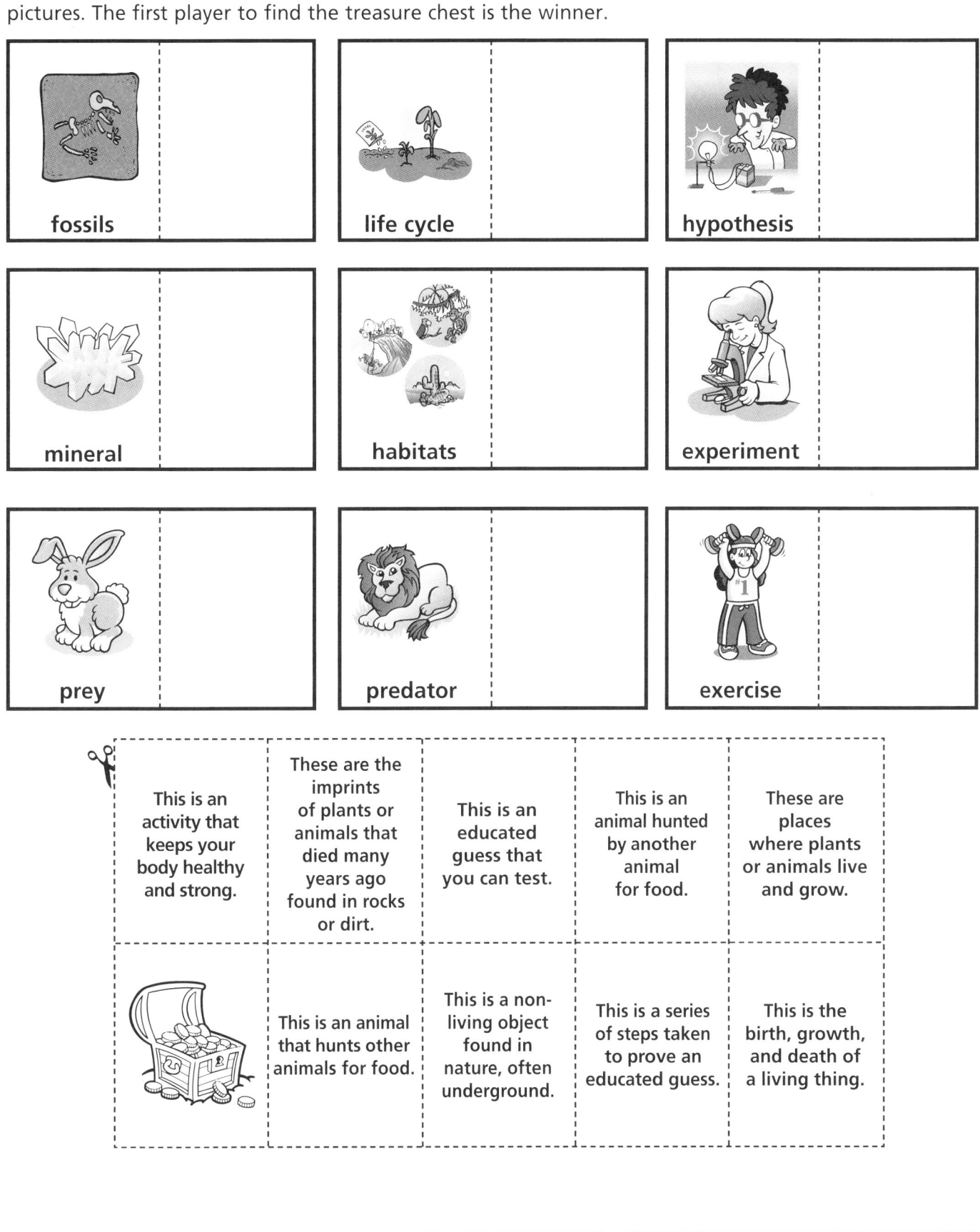

fossils	life cycle	hypothesis
mineral	habitats	experiment
prey	predator	exercise

This is an activity that keeps your body healthy and strong.	These are the imprints of plants or animals that died many years ago found in rocks or dirt.	This is an educated guess that you can test.	This is an animal hunted by another animal for food.	These are places where plants or animals live and grow.
(treasure chest)	This is an animal that hunts other animals for food.	This is a non-living object found in nature, often underground.	This is a series of steps taken to prove an educated guess.	This is the birth, growth, and death of a living thing.

_____   _____   _____
Name   Date   Helper

#BKCRD-56 Core Curriculum Vocab Cards Fun Sheets – Level 2 • ©2012 Super Duper® Publications • www.superduperinc.com

55

Science – What's the Correct Meaning?

Directions: Read each sentence. Circle the picture and definition on the right that have the correct meaning for the word in bold.

1. A good example of **cause and effect** is freezing water into ice.

   This is a series of steps taken to prove an educated guess.

   This is when one event happens and another event results from it.

2. We are expecting up to three inches of **precipitation** this evening.

   This is water, rain, snow, or hail falling from the sky.

   This is the process of a gas changing into a liquid.

3. The **evaporation** of the ocean water left only salt crystals in our pan.

   This is the process of a liquid changing into a gas.

   These are the smallest parts of living things.

4. The teacher had us **classify** the different rocks according to their makeup.

   This is an animal hunted by another animal for food.

   This is when you sort objects or living things into groups.

5. One part of our project is to **observe** the different phases of the moon each night.

   This is the name for a living plant or animal.

   This is when you watch something carefully and gather information about it.

6. If everyone learned to **recycle** their trash, it would help preserve our natural resources.

   This means to create something new from used material.

   This is the birth, growth, and death of a living thing.

_____ _____ _____
Name   Date   Helper

Science – What's the Correct Meaning?

Directions: Read each sentence. Circle the picture and definition on the right that have the correct meaning for the word in bold.

1. The pull of the **magnet** in the door's frame helps keep the door closed.

   This is the act of moving from one place to another.

   This is a solid object that attracts metal objects. 

2. We could see the shape of an animal as we studied the huge **cloud**.

   This is a non-living object found in nature, often underground.

   This is a collection of water or ice droplets in the sky that you can see. 

3. The **atmosphere** surrounding Earth can be divided into several layers.

   This is made up of the invisible gases that surround Earth.

   These are the imprints of plants or animals that died many years ago found in rocks or dirt. 

4. The earth will **rotate** one time in 24 hours.

   This means to create something new from used material.

   This means to turn around and around on a center point or axis. 

5. When Beth put the car in **motion**, we were off to the movies.

   This is the act of moving from one place to another.

   This is an animal that hunts other animals for food. 

6. We use **fossils** to learn about the animals that lived long ago.

   These are the imprints of plants or animals that died many years ago found in rocks or dirt.

   This is a non-living object found in nature, often underground. 

Name   Date   Helper

Science – What's the Correct Meaning?

Directions: Read each sentence. Circle the picture and definition on the right that have the correct meaning for the word in bold.

1. Gold and silver are very valuable **minerals**.

   This is a solid object that attracts metal objects.

   This is a non-living object found in nature, often underground.

2. We watched the hawk fly as it searched for its **prey**.

   This is when you sort objects or living things into groups.

   This is an animal hunted by another animal for food.

3. For some animals, a human is their worst **predator**.

   These are the imprints of plants or animals that died many years ago found in rocks or dirt.

   This is an animal that hunts other animals for food.

4. The **life cycle** of a queen honey bee lasts as long as three years.

   This is the birth, growth, and death of a living thing.

   This is when one event happens and another event results from it.

5. Some animals would not be able to survive in other animals' **habitats**.

   This is made up of the invisible gases that surround Earth.

   These are places where plants or animals live and grow.

6. We proved our hypothesis true by conducting an **experiment**.

   This is a series of steps taken to prove an educated guess.

   This is when you watch something carefully and gather information about it.

Name   Date   Helper

Science – Answer It!

Directions: Read each question. Then put an X on the letter next to the picture and vocabulary word that best answers the question.

1. What can you do to prove that a scientific guess is true?

   A) cause and effect   B) experiment

---

2. What can you do to keep your body healthy and strong?

   A) precipitation   B) exercise

---

3. Which describes the water on the outside of your windows in the morning?

   A) condensation   B) weather

---

4. What is another name for an animal or plant?

   A) organism   B) evaporation

---

5. What can you do to learn more about something that interests you?

   A) classify   B) investigate

---

6. Which are the smallest parts of your body?

   A) cells   B) fossils

Name   Date   Helper

Science – Answer It!

Directions: Read each question. Then put an X on the letter next to the picture and vocabulary word that best answers the question.

1. Which describes a snowfall?

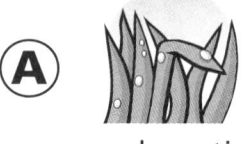

    A. condensation
    B. precipitation

2. What describes throwing a ball toward a window and breaking it?

    A. cause and effect
    B. magnet

3. Which describes a puddle of water that dried up?

    A. evaporation
    B. hypothesis

4. What do we do to sort things with similar features?

    A. classify
    B. experiment

5. Which hunts other animals for food?

    A. prey
    B. predator

6. Which names and describes movement?

    A. motion
    B. recycle

Name _____ Date _____ Helper _____

Science – Answer It!

Directions: Read each question. Then put an X on the letter next to the picture and vocabulary word that best answers the question.

1. What can attract other metal objects to itself?

    A) magnet   B) hypothesis

---

2. Which describes water in the sky that you can see?

    A) atmosphere   B) cloud

---

3. What is another word to describe "turn"?

    A) motion   B) rotate

---

4. What helps us learn about animals that lived long ago?

    A) observe   B) fossils

---

5. Which describes a rock or non-living object found underground?

    A) mineral   B) life cycle

---

6. What describes the wind, temperature, rainfall, and clouds at any particular place or time?

    A) evaporation   B) weather

Name	Date	Helper

Science – Sentence Completion

Directions: Read each sentence below. Complete each sentence using a vocabulary word from the Word/Picture Bank. Write the word in the blank.

Word/Picture Bank

cause and effect	life cycle	observe	atmosphere	weather
habitats	hypothesis	recycle	prey	exercise

1. The layers of our _____ help protect us from some of the sun's dangerous rays.

2. We _____ every day in gym class.

3. If everyone would _____, our natural resources would last much longer.

4. A good example of _____ is applying heat to water to make it boil.

5. The _____ of an ant is very short.

6. We must _____ a caterpillar turning into a butterfly for our project.

7. The _____ should be perfect for a picnic tomorrow.

8. We watched the hawk soar through the sky searching for its _____.

9. The animals' _____ at the zoo are similar to the places where they live in the wild.

10. My _____ is that my garden will not grow if I water it with very salty water.

_____ _____ _____
Name   Date   Helper

Science – Sentence Completion

Directions: Read each sentence below. Complete each sentence using a vocabulary word from the Word/Picture Bank. Write the word in the blank.

Word/Picture Bank

precipitation	fossils	rotate	cloud	condensation
mineral	cells	organism	investigate	magnet

1. The _____ that fell last night totaled two inches.

2. Which _____ is strong enough to pick up these heavy nails?

3. How do _____ work when they are so very tiny?

4. The scientists used _____ to rebuild what was once a dinosaur.

5. How does Earth _____ on its axis without falling over?

6. The _____ covered the grass in our yard this morning.

7. Every living _____ needs air, food, and water.

8. Our assignment was to _____ the insects and write a report about each one.

9. The large puffy _____ in the sky looked like an animal.

10. Gold is a very valuable _____ used to make expensive jewelry.

_____ _____ _____
Name   Date   Helper

Science – Sentence Completion

Directions: Read each sentence below. Complete each sentence using a vocabulary word from the Word/Picture Bank. Write the word in the blank.

Word/Picture Bank

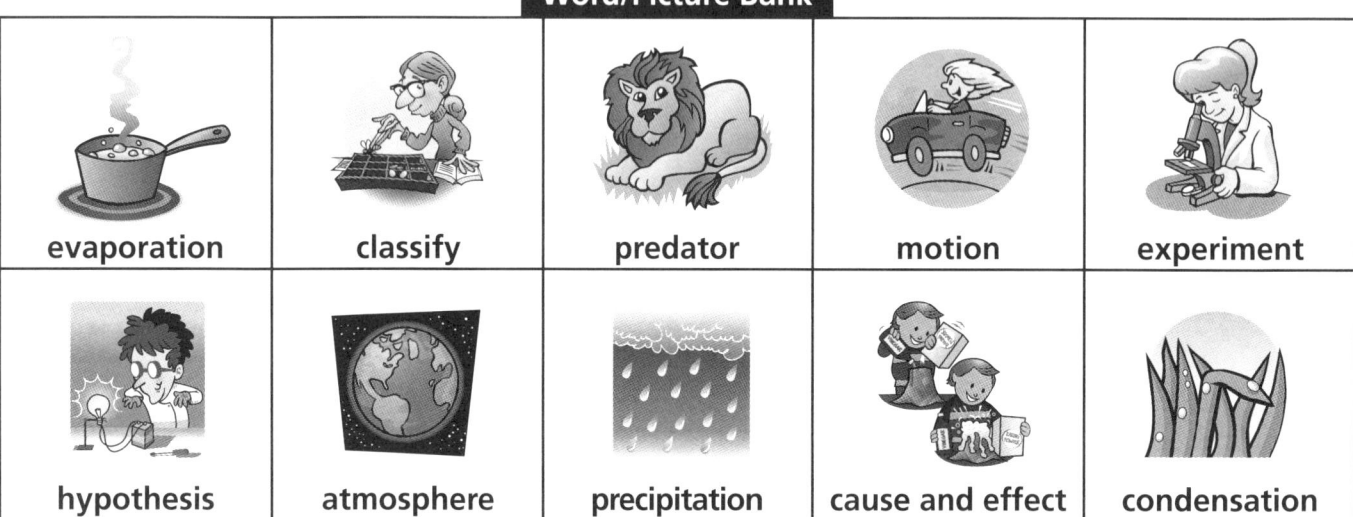

| evaporation | classify | predator | motion | experiment |
| hypothesis | atmosphere | precipitation | cause and effect | condensation |

1. The _____ proved to be true once we performed the experiment to test it.

2. We could see a blaze of light as the space shuttle entered Earth's _____ .

3. Adding vinegar to baking soda and it bubbling is an example of _____ .

4. A _____ hunts continuously for its prey.

5. The teacher asked us to _____ the items as living or non-living.

6. The day was so hot that _____ ran down the side of my cold glass.

7. Once the car was in _____ , we realized we needed gas.

8. We performed an _____ to prove that our hypothesis was correct.

9. The weatherman is predicting _____ in the form of snow and sleet.

10. The quick _____ of all the water from the soil caused the flowers to die.

_____   _____   _____
Name   Date   Helper

Science – Which Ones Belong Together?

Directions: Cut out the three pictures in Row 1. Glue the two pictures that go together in the empty boxes on the left. Tell why the two pictures go together. Complete the page one row at a time.

1.	condensation	fossils	precipitation
2.	organism	cells	exercise
3.	investigate	predator	prey
4.	recycle	hypothesis	experiment
5.	mineral	fossils	cloud
6.	rotate	cloud	precipitation

Name   Date   Helper

Science – Which Doesn't Belong?

Directions: Read/Listen carefully to each group of words. Mark an X through the word that doesn't belong. Tell how the other words relate to each other.

1. motion, fossils, cells, organism

2. atmosphere, cloud, exercise, weather

3. condensation, evaporation, cause and effect, cells

4. predator, magnet, prey, life cycle

5. experiment, hypothesis, rotate, cause and effect

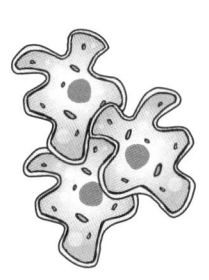

6. precipitation, mineral, condensation, evaporation

7. habitats, experiment, prey, predator

8. cloud, observe, experiment, hypothesis

9. exercise, prey, life cycle, organism

10. mineral, fossil, recycle, organism

Science – Which Doesn't Belong?

Directions: Put an X through the picture in each row that doesn't belong. Tell why the other two pictures belong together.

1. mineral | predator | prey

2. classify | rotate | motion

3. hypothesis | experiment | recycle

4. observe | cells | organism

5. precipitation | recycle | cloud

6. mineral | cause and effect | organism

_____   _____   _____
Name   Date   Helper

Science – Say It, Paste It - Initial

Directions: Have the student cut out the pictures at the bottom of the page. The helper names a picture aloud, then the student glues/tapes or places it on the big picture with the same *beginning* sound.

Name | Date | Helper

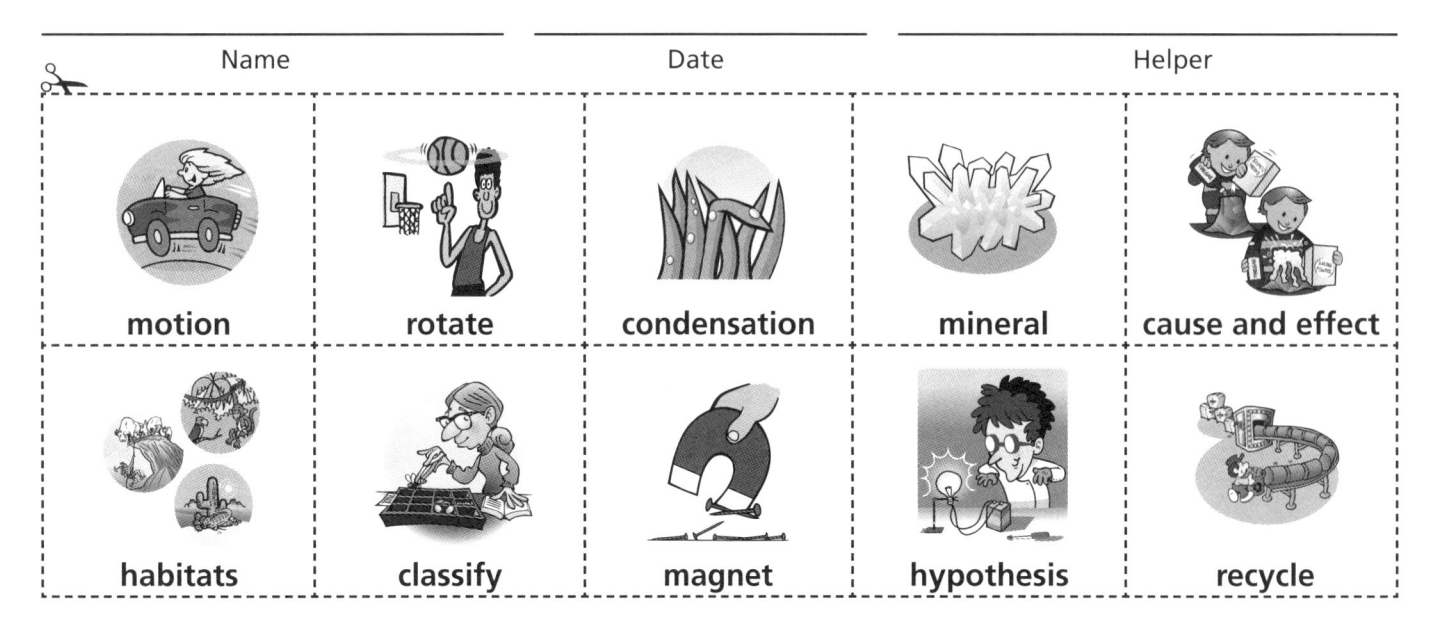

motion | rotate | condensation | mineral | cause and effect

habitats | classify | magnet | hypothesis | recycle

Science – Say It, Paste It - Final

Directions: Have the student cut out the pictures at the bottom of the page. The helper names a picture aloud, then the student glues/tapes or places it on the big picture with the same *ending* sound.

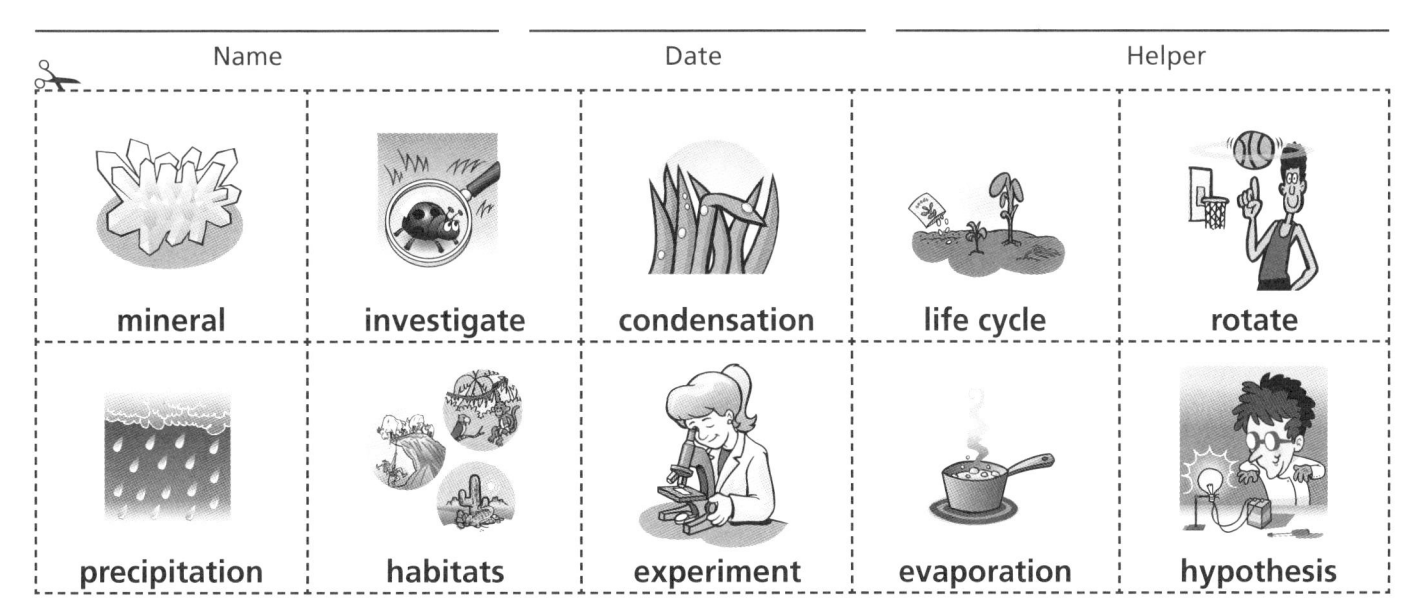

Name _____ Date _____ Helper _____

mineral	investigate	condensation	life cycle	rotate
precipitation	habitats	experiment	evaporation	hypothesis

Science – Breakdown

Directions: Have the students cut out the pictures. The student names each picture aloud and counts how many syllables (or parts of the word) it has. The student glues/tapes or places the picture on the side of the page with that number of syllables.

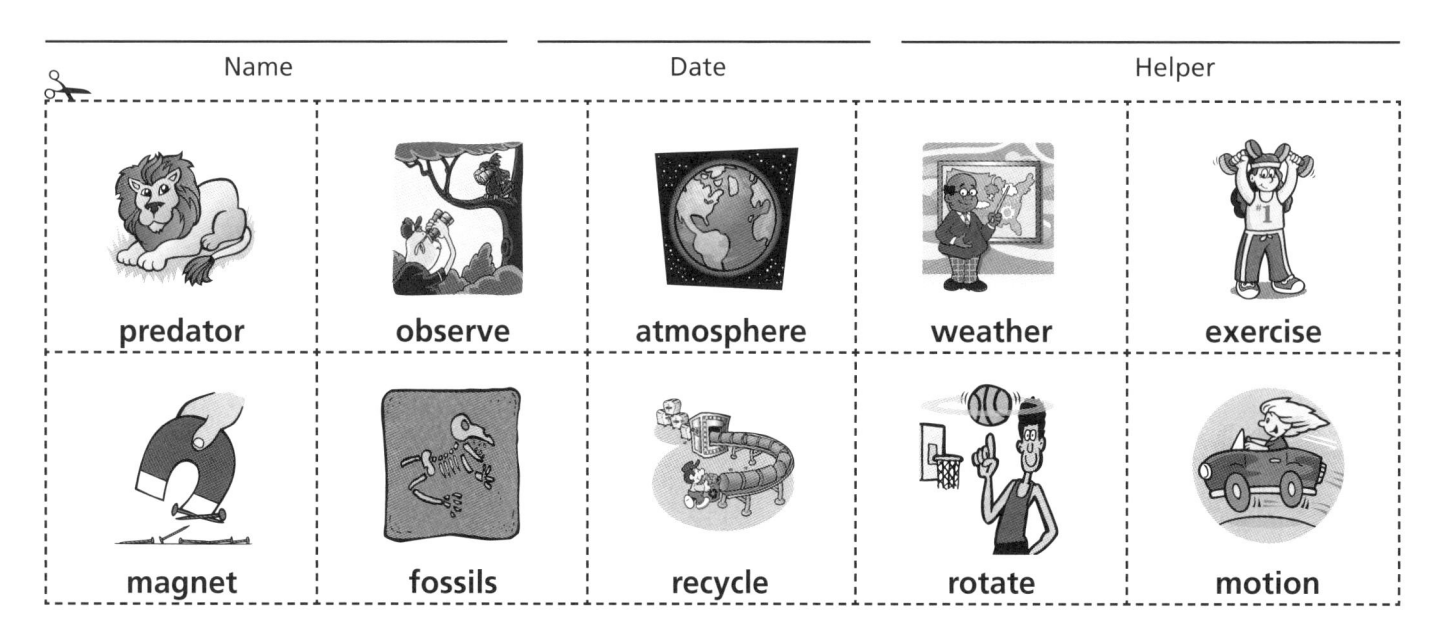

2 syllables	3 syllables

Name _____ Date _____ Helper _____

predator	observe	atmosphere	weather	exercise
magnet	fossils	recycle	rotate	motion

Science – Syllable Search

Directions: Have the students cut out the pictures. The student names each picture aloud and counts how many syllables (or parts of the word) it has. The student glues/tapes or places the picture on the side of the page with that number of syllables. Have the student find the two words that don't belong and tell the number of syllables they have.

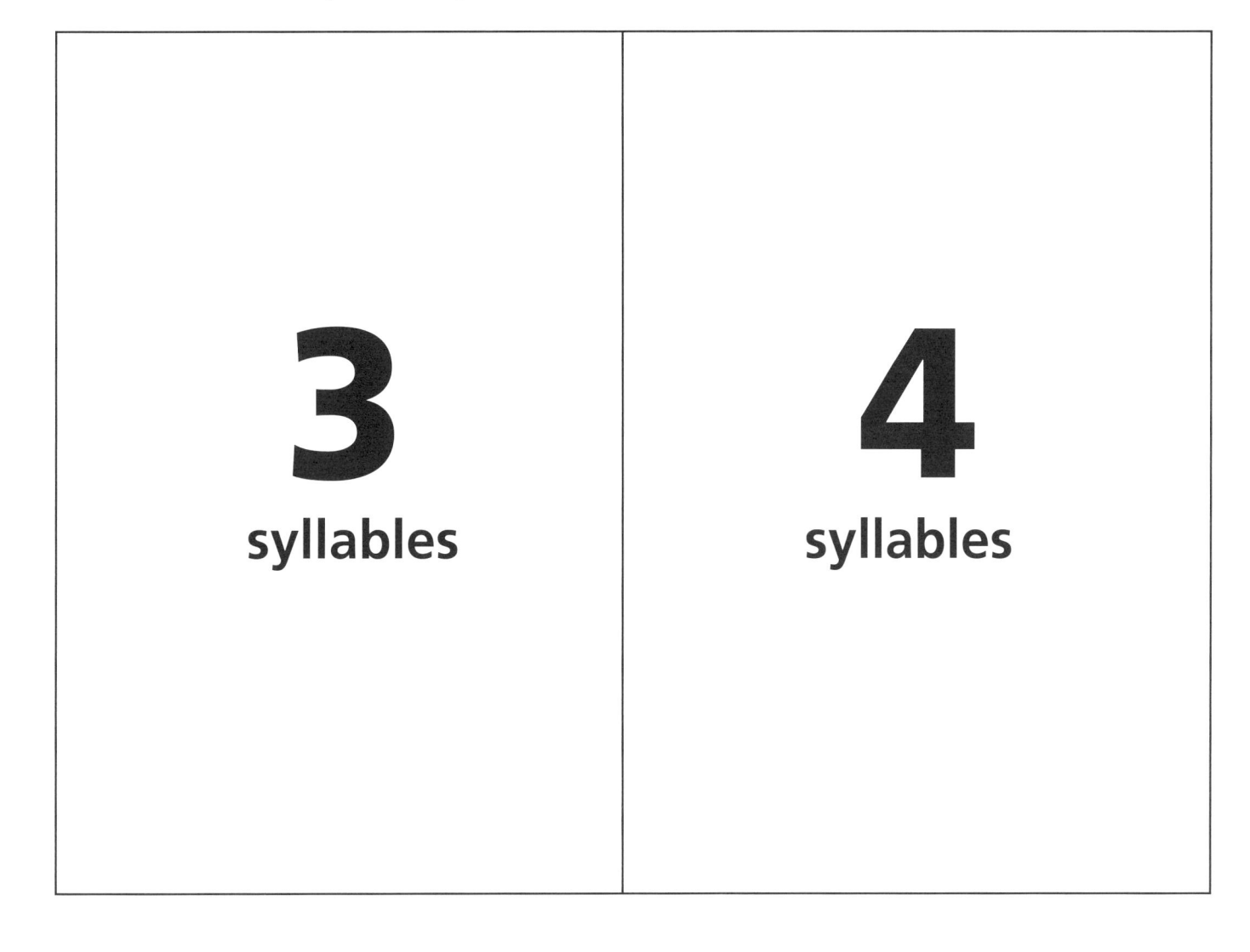

3 syllables	4 syllables

Name | Date | Helper

experiment	evaporation	habitats	precipitation	condensation
hypothesis	classify	investigate	life cycle	mineral

Science – Word Scramble Riddle

Directions: Unscramble the words to name each picture and write the letters in the blanks. Then take the letters in the circles and write them in order in the blanks at the bottom of the page to answer the riddle.

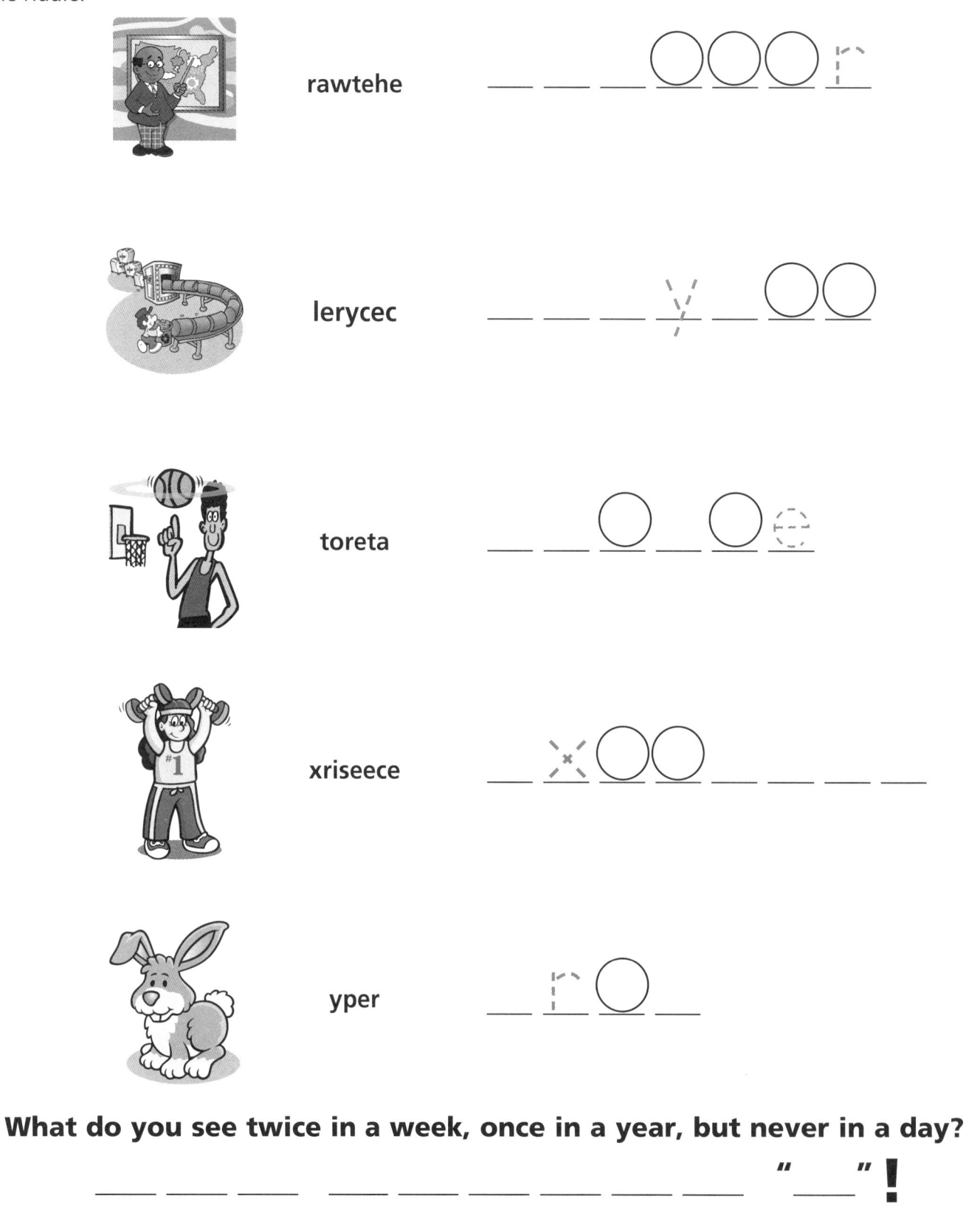

rawtehe

lerycec

toreta

xriseece

yper

What do you see twice in a week, once in a year, but never in a day?

___ ___ ___ ___ ___ ___ ___ ___ ___ "___"!

Science – Word Scramble Riddle

Directions: Unscramble the words to name each picture and write the letters in the blanks. Then take the letters in the circles and write them in order in the blanks at the bottom of the page to answer the riddle.

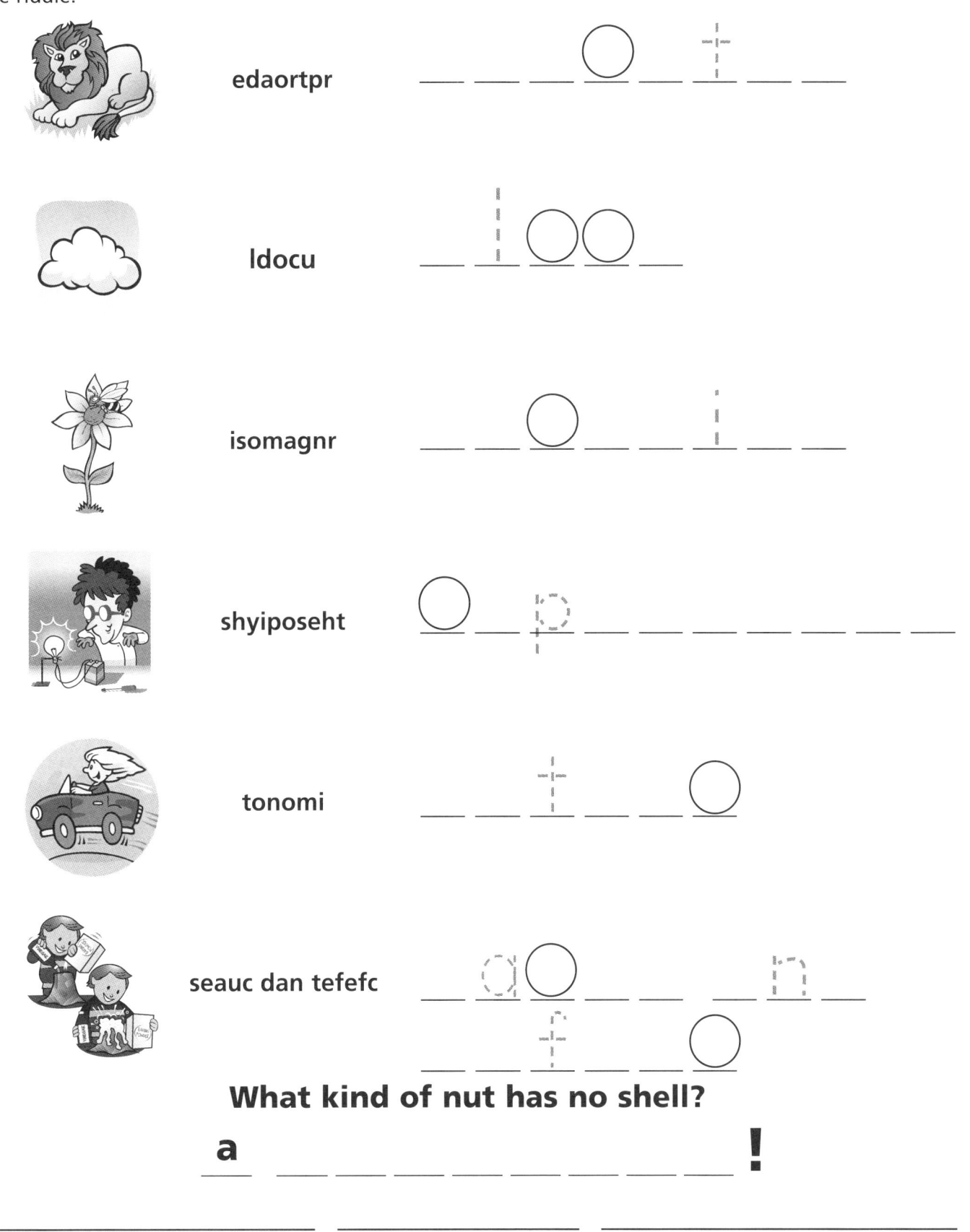

edaortpr __ __ __ __ Ⓞ __t__

ldocu __ __i__ Ⓞ Ⓞ

isomagnr __ __ Ⓞ __ __ __i__

shyiposeht Ⓞ __ Ⓞ __ __ __ __ __ __

tonomi __ __ __t__ Ⓞ

seauc dan tefefc __ Ⓞ __ __ __ __ __n__
__ __t__ __ Ⓞ

What kind of nut has no shell?

a __ __ __ __ __ __ __ __ __ !

Name / Date / Helper

Science – Word Scramble Riddle

Directions: Unscramble the words to name each picture and write the letters in the blanks. Then take the letters in the circles and write them in order in the blanks at the bottom of the page to answer the riddle.

rewhaet ◯ __ __ t ◯ __ __

tetroa __ o __ ◯ ◯ __

thepoyhssi __ __ p __ ◯ __ __ __ ◯ __

spomtarehe __ __ ◯ __ __ __ h ◯ __ __

silfoss __ __ s __ ◯ __ ◯

gnvsietiate ◯ __ v __ __ ◯ __ __ __ __

What question do people ask all day long and get a different answer each time, yet all the answers are correct?

__ __ __ __   __ __ __ __ __   __ __   __ __ ?

Name　　　　　Date　　　　　Helper

74

Science – Writing Definitions

Directions: Read the vocabulary words below each picture. Then write a sentence beside each picture using the vocabulary word. Use the definition clues at the bottom of the page to help you.

1. recycle

2. exercise

3. prey

4. predator

5. cloud

6. organism

an activity that keeps your body healthy and strong	an animal hunted by another animal for food	to create something new from used material
an animal that hunts other animals for food	a collection of water or ice droplets in the sky that you can see	the name for a living plant or animal

Name   Date   Helper

Science – Writing Definitions

Directions: Read the vocabulary words below each picture. Then write a sentence beside each picture using the vocabulary word. Use the definition clues at the bottom of the page to help you.

1. motion

2. cause and effect

3. cells

4. observe

5. evaporation

6. condensation

when one event happens and another event results from it	moving from one place to another	watching something carefully and gathering information about it
the process of a liquid changing into a gas	the process of a gas changing into a liquid	the smallest parts of living things

_____ _____ _____
Name   Date   Helper

76

Science – Writing Definitions

Directions: Read the vocabulary words below each picture. Then write a sentence beside each picture using the vocabulary word. Use the definition clues at the bottom of the page to help you.

1. investigate _____

2. experiment _____

3. mineral _____

4. habitats _____

5. life cycle _____

6. classify _____

a series of steps taken to prove an educated guess	places where plants or animals live and grow	a non-living object found in nature, often underground
the birth, growth, and death of a living thing	sorting objects or living things into groups	studying something closely to learn facts or information about it

_____   _____   _____
Name   Date   Helper

Science – Writing Definitions

Directions: Read the vocabulary words below each picture. Then write a sentence beside each picture using the vocabulary word. Use the definition clues at the bottom of the page to help you.

1. atmosphere

2. precipitation

3. rotate

4. weather

5. hypothesis

6. fossils

an educated guess that you can test	the imprints of plants or animals that died many years ago found in rocks or dirt	turning around and around on a center point or axis
the wind, temperature, rainfall, and clouds in a particular place and time	the invisible gases that surround Earth	water, rain, snow, or hail falling from the sky

Name   Date   Helper

Social Studies – Definition Match-Up

Directions: Draw a line from the definition in Column A to the word that matches it in Column B. Read/Say the definition and its matching vocabulary word aloud.

A

- This is something found in nature such as water, trees, and minerals that people need and use.
- This is the name for shared beliefs and behaviors of a group of people.
- These are things that are bought or sold.
- This is a group of people about the same age and growing up around the same time.
- This is a made-up story that people have told over and over throughout the ages.
- This is a family member who lived before you did.

B

- generation
- natural resource
- ancestor
- folktale
- culture
- goods

_____ _____ _____
Name   Date   Helper

Social Studies – Star Match-Up

Directions: Cut out the definitions at the bottom of the page. Shuffle the definitions and place them facedown. Have the students take turns reading the definitions and placing them next to the correct pictures. The first player to find the star is the winner.

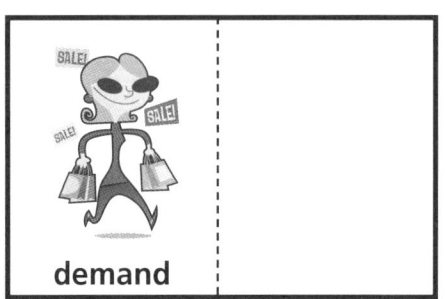

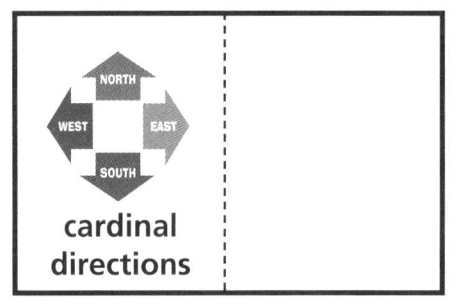

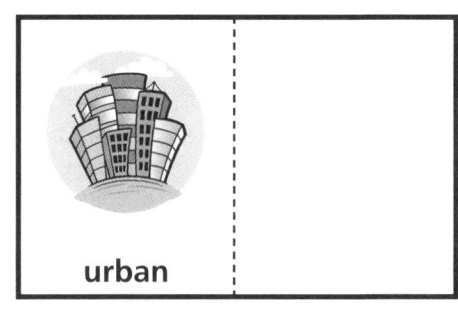

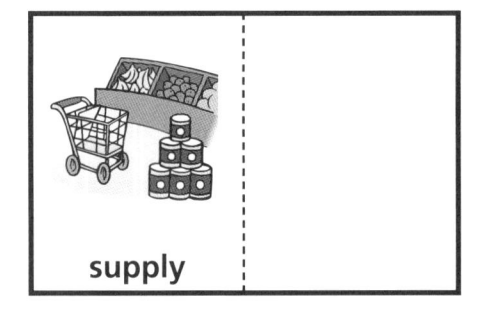

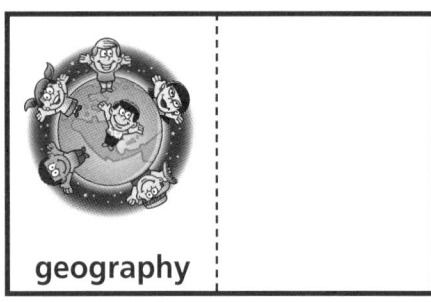

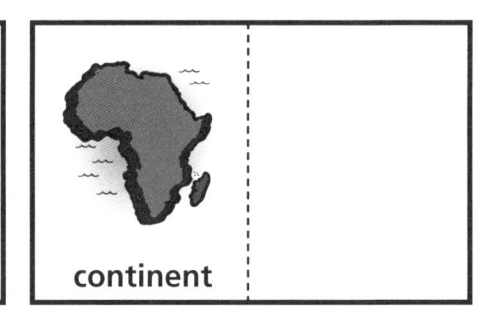

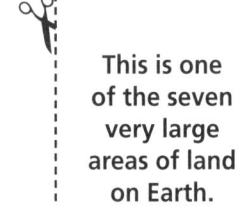

service	demand	compass rose
trade	cardinal directions	urban
supply	geography	continent

This is one of the seven very large areas of land on Earth.	This is a symbol on a map that shows north, south, east, and west.	This is what you call something that has to do with the city.	This is a word for buying and selling things.	This is what you call north, south, east, and west.
★	This is how much of something people want to buy.	This is something that helps people or gives them what they want.	This is the study of the world's surface, its climate, and peoples.	This is how many items are available for people to buy.

Name　　　　　Date　　　　　Helper

Social Studies – Treasure Chest Match-Up

Directions: Cut out the definitions at the bottom of the page. Shuffle the definitions and place them facedown. Have the students take turns reading the definitions and placing them next to the correct pictures. The first player to find the treasure chest is the winner.

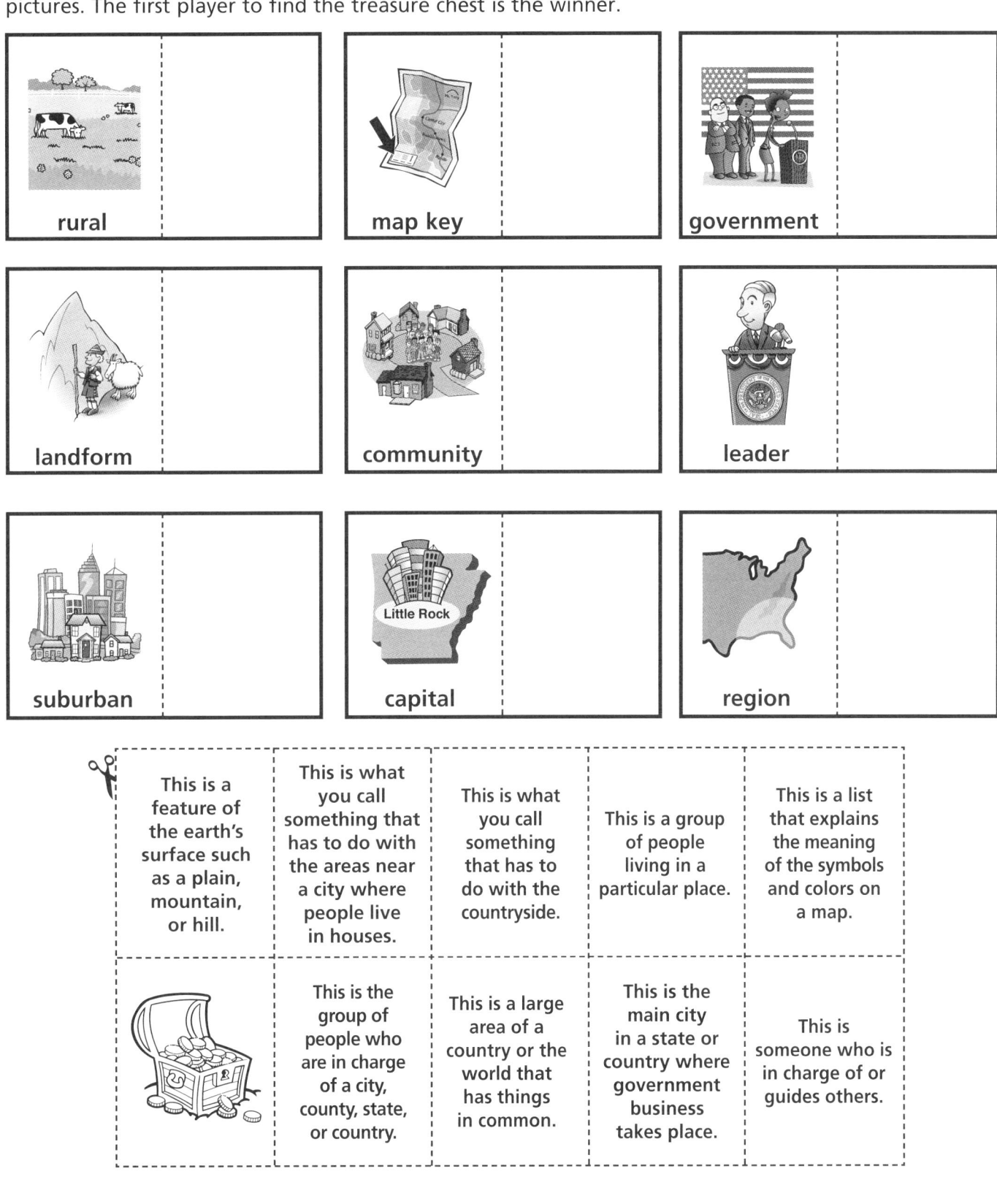

rural	map key	government
landform	community	leader
suburban	capital	region

This is a feature of the earth's surface such as a plain, mountain, or hill.	This is what you call something that has to do with the areas near a city where people live in houses.	This is what you call something that has to do with the countryside.	This is a group of people living in a particular place.	This is a list that explains the meaning of the symbols and colors on a map.
(treasure chest)	This is the group of people who are in charge of a city, county, state, or country.	This is a large area of a country or the world that has things in common.	This is the main city in a state or country where government business takes place.	This is someone who is in charge of or guides others.

Name _____ Date _____ Helper _____

#BKCRD-56 Core Curriculum Vocab Cards Fun Sheets – Level 2 • ©2012 Super Duper® Publications • www.superduperinc.com

Social Studies – What's the Correct Meaning?

Directions: Read each sentence. Circle the picture and definition on the right that have the correct meaning for the word in bold.

1. According to the **timeline**, when was the Declaration of Independence signed?

   This is a symbol on a map that shows north, south, east, and west.

   This is a display that shows when certain events happened over a period of time.

2. George Washington is one of my **ancestors**.

   This is someone who is in charge of or guides others.

   This is a family member who lived before you did.

3. In our **culture**, men and women have equal rights under the law.

   This is the name for shared beliefs and behaviors of a group of people.

   This is how much of something people want to buy.

4. Grandpa's **generation** was the first to see men walk on the moon.

   This is a family member who lived before you did.

   This is a group of people about the same age and growing up around the same time.

5. Have you ever heard the **folktale** about Paul Bunyan and his blue ox?

   This is a display that shows when certain events happened over a period of time.

   This is a made-up story that people have told over and over throughout the ages.

6. Is there a plentiful **supply** of sleds to purchase before the snow falls?

   This is how many items are available for people to buy.

   This is something that helps people or gives them what they want.

Name _____ Date _____ Helper _____

Social Studies – What's the Correct Meaning?

Directions: Read each sentence. Circle the picture and definition on the right that have the correct meaning for the word in bold.

1. Mason's Market has a variety of **goods** that were made in Japan.

   These are things that are bought or sold.

   This is a word for buying and selling things.

2. Wood is a very valuable **natural resource**.

   This is how many items are available for people to buy.

   This is something found in nature such as water, trees, and minerals that people need and use.

3. The staff at Mac's Diner provides excellent **service** to their customers.

   This is something that helps people or gives them what they want.

   This is how much of something people want to buy.

4. Our country must **trade** with other countries to get things we don't have here.

   This is a word for buying and selling things.

   This is a group of people about the same age and growing up around the same time.

5. The **demand** for swimsuits is very low when the weather is cold.

   This is how much of something people want to buy.

   This is someone who is in charge of or guides others.

6. The compass rose on my map displays all the **cardinal directions**.

   This is what you call north, south, east, and west.

   This is a group of people living in a particular place.

_____ _____ _____
Name   Date   Helper

83

Social Studies – What's the Correct Meaning?

Directions: Read each sentence. Circle the picture and definition on the right that have the correct meaning for the word in bold.

1. Many maps have a **compass rose** showing the cardinal directions.

   This is the group of people who are in charge of a city, county, state, or country.

   This is a symbol on a map that shows north, south, east, and west.

2. On which **continent** will you find the country of Mexico?

   This is one of the seven very large areas of land on Earth.

   This is a feature of the earth's surface such as a plain, mountain, or hill.

3. The **geography** of the land is very rocky and flat.

   This is a large area of a country or the world that has things in common.

   This is the study of the world's surface, its climate, and peoples.

4. Many people commute to **urban** areas to work each day.

   This is what you call something that has to do with the city.

   This is a group of people about the same age and growing up around the same time.

5. **Suburban** areas outside the city have many neighborhoods and communities.

   This is a large area of a country or the world that has things in common.

   This is what you call something that has to do with the areas near a city where people live in houses.

6. You can find many farms in the **rural** areas of our state.

   This is what you call something that has to do with the countryside.

   This is a group of people living in a particular place.

_____   _____   _____
Name   Date   Helper

84   #BKCRD-56 Core Curriculum Vocab Cards Fun Sheets – Level 2 • ©2012 Super Duper® Publications • www.superduperinc.com

Social Studies – Answer It!

Directions: Read each question. Then put an X on the letter next to the picture and vocabulary word that best answers the question.

1. Who is in charge of guiding others in the business of government?

   A) leader   B) ancestor

2. What kind of story has been made up and told throughout the ages?

   A) timeline   B) folktale

3. Which group of people are about the same age and grew up around the same time?

   A) government   B) generation

4. What group of people conducts the business of a city, state, or country?

   A) government   B) map key

5. Where does the state's government business take place?

   A) trade   B) capital

6. What part of a map displays and explains the meaning of its symbols?

   A) map key   B) compass rose

_____   _____   _____
Name   Date   Helper

Social Studies – Answer It!

Directions: Read each question. Then put an X on the letter next to the picture and vocabulary word that best answers the question.

1. Where do many families live?

   A) geography
   B) community

2. Which displays cardinal directions?

   A) compass rose
   B) timeline

3. What is a large area where people have many things in common?

   A) ancestor
   B) region

4. What describes the surface of the earth?

   A) geography
   B) natural resource

5. Which term refers to something about a city?

   A) rural
   B) urban

6. Which term refers to areas outside the city where people live mostly in houses?

   A) suburban
   B) culture

_____   _____   _____
Name   Date   Helper

Social Studies – Answer It!

Directions: Read each question. Then put an X on the letter next to the picture and vocabulary word that best answers the question.

1. What things do you buy and sell?

    A) goods   B) leader

2. What is something found in nature people need and use?

    A) trade   B) natural resource

3. What is the number of items available for people to buy?

    A) folktale   B) supply

4. What tells how much of something people want to buy?

    A) demand   B) ancestor

5. What describes the beliefs and behaviors shared among a group of people?

    A) region   B) culture

6. Who is someone in your family that lived long ago?

    A) ancestor   B) generation

_____ _____ _____
Name   Date   Helper

Social Studies – Sentence Completion

Directions: Read each sentence below. Complete each sentence using a vocabulary word from the Word/Picture Bank. Write the word in the blank.

Word/Picture Bank

continent	timeline	cardinal directions	trade	landform
service	compass rose	community	map key	capital

1. The _____ shows that Alaska became a state a year before Hawaii.

2. The _____ of North America lies above the equator.

3. The Grand Canyon is a major _____ in the United States.

4. The neighbors in our _____ are planning a picnic.

5. Grandpa prefers to _____ with local grocery stores near his home.

6. Looking at the map's _____, Montana is to the north of Wyoming.

7. Robb's Garage provides excellent _____ to his customers.

8. North, south, east, and west are _____.

9. We used the _____ to figure out what the star on the map means.

10. Our nation's business takes place in the _____ of Washington, D.C.

_____   _____   _____
Name   Date   Helper

Social Studies – Sentence Completion

Directions: Read each sentence below. Complete each sentence using a vocabulary word from the Word/Picture Bank. Write the word in the blank.

Word/Picture Bank

government	suburban	rural	leader	urban
generation	folktale	geography	region	culture

1. The _____ of our state varies from flat beaches to high mountains.

2. Our _____ has been using computers and other technology for years.

3. Which _____ of the United States includes Florida?

4. _____ areas have restaurants and convenience stores between skyscrapers.

5. The state _____ passed a new speed limit law for our highways.

6. Who is the _____ of your state government?

7. You will see many barns and pastures in the _____ areas of the state.

8. I live in a _____ area just outside the city.

9. Mom used to read me the _____ about John-Henry, the steel-driving man.

10. Each country throughout the world has its own _____ or beliefs about their way of doing things.

_____   _____   _____
Name   Date   Helper

Social Studies – Sentence Completion

Directions: Read each sentence below. Complete each sentence using a vocabulary word from the Word/Picture Bank. Write the word in the blank.

Word/Picture Bank

demand	goods	service	landform	continent
natural resource	ancestor	trade	supply	timeline

1. The _____ for snow shovels rises in winter months.

2. Use the _____ to see what year Abe Lincoln became president.

3. Local citizens _____ with stores in our community rather than going shopping at the mall.

4. Clean water is a very valuable _____.

5. One famous _____ in my family was Albert Einstein.

6. The stores have a huge _____ of wrapping paper in December.

7. Only scientists conducting research live on the _____ of Antarctica.

8. The city's mall carries a variety of _____ made here in our state.

9. Police officers provide an extra _____ to our community by patrolling our streets at night.

10. Mount Everest is a large, natural _____.

_____ _____ _____
Name   Date   Helper

Social Studies – Which Ones Belong Together?

Directions: Cut out the three pictures in Row 1. Glue the two pictures that go together in the empty boxes on the left. Tell why the two pictures go together. Complete the page one row at a time.

1.

2.

3.

4.

5.

6.

1. cardinal directions | timeline | compass rose

2. folktale | government | capital

3. rural | suburban | culture

4. landform | trade | geography

5. natural resource | supply | demand

6. goods | service | generation

Name _____ Date _____ Helper _____

#BKCRD-56 *Core Curriculum Vocab Cards Fun Sheets – Level 2* • ©2012 Super Duper® Publications • www.superduperinc.com

91

Social Studies – Which Doesn't Belong?

Directions: Read/Listen carefully to each group of words. Mark an X through the word that doesn't belong. Tell how the other words relate to each other.

1. compass rose, generation, map key, cardinal directions

2. timeline, rural, suburban, urban

3. landform, natural resource, geography, folktale

4. goods, service, culture, supply

5. leader, folktale, government, capital

6. trade, urban, supply, demand

7. generation, community, culture, continent

8. cardinal directions, landform, compass rose, map key

9. continent, region, capital, ancestor

10. service, goods, timeline, trade

Social Studies – Which Doesn't Belong?

Directions: Put an X through the picture in each row that doesn't belong. Tell why the other two pictures belong together.

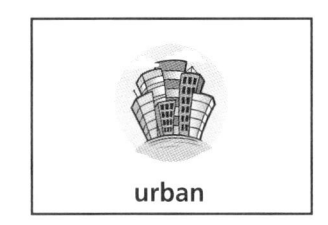

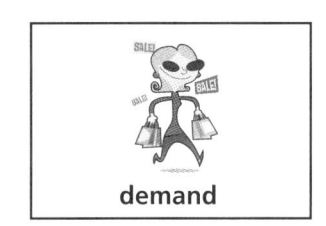

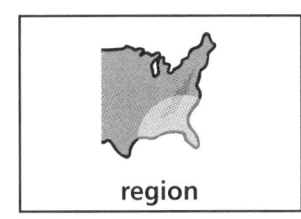

1. service | goods | community

2. capital | government | urban

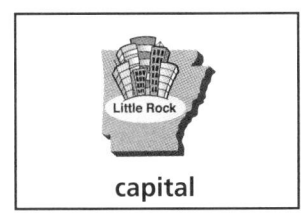

3. culture | supply | demand

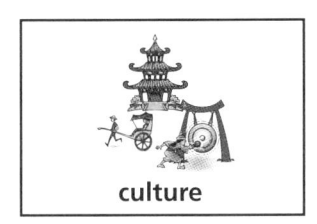

4. generation | government | leader

5. suburban | region | rural

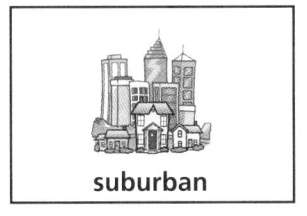

6. map key | ancestor | compass rose

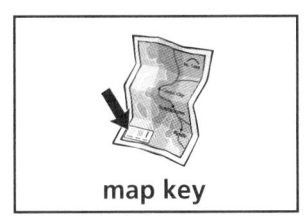

_____ _____ _____
Name   Date   Helper

Social Studies – Say It, Paste It - Initial

Directions: Have the student cut out the pictures at the bottom of the page. The helper names a picture aloud, then the student glues/tapes or places it on the big picture with the same *beginning* sound.

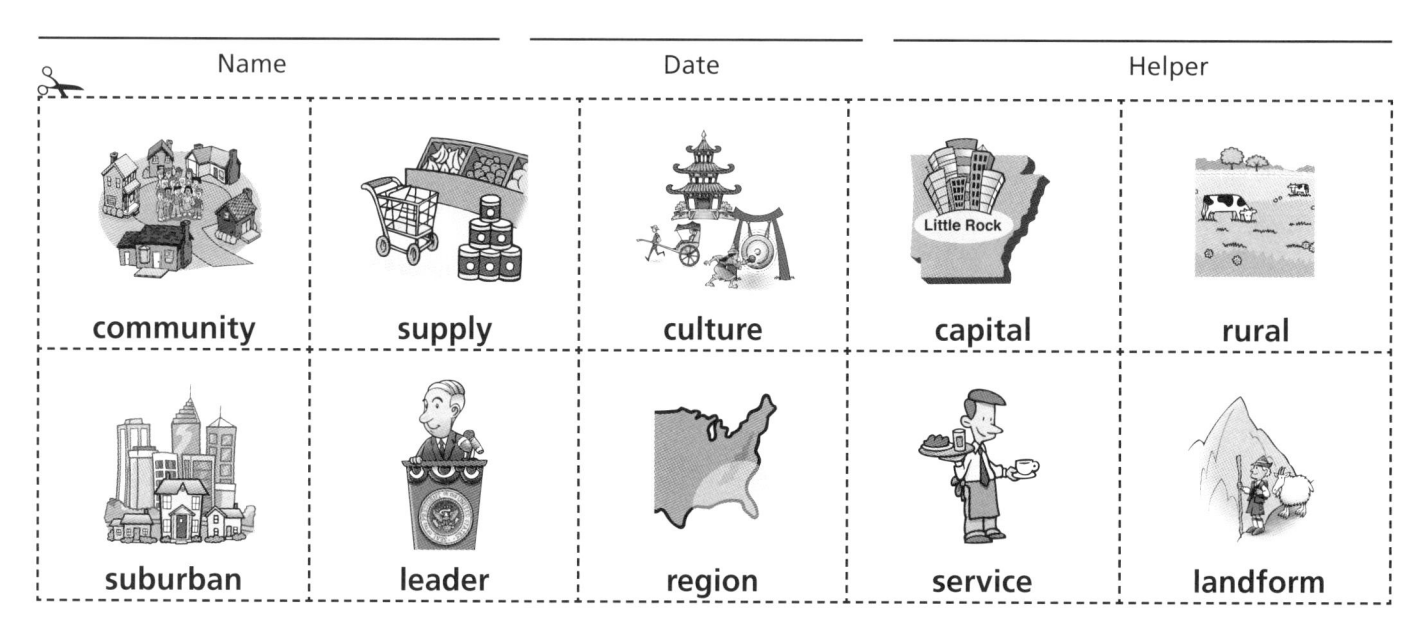

Name	Date	Helper

community	supply	culture	capital	rural
suburban	leader	region	service	landform

94 #BKCRD-56 Core Curriculum Vocab Cards Fun Sheets – Level 2 • ©2012 Super Duper® Publications • www.superduperinc.com

Social Studies – Say It, Paste It - Final

Directions: Have the student cut out the pictures at the bottom of the page. The helper names a picture aloud, then the student glues/tapes or places it on the big picture with the same *ending* sound.

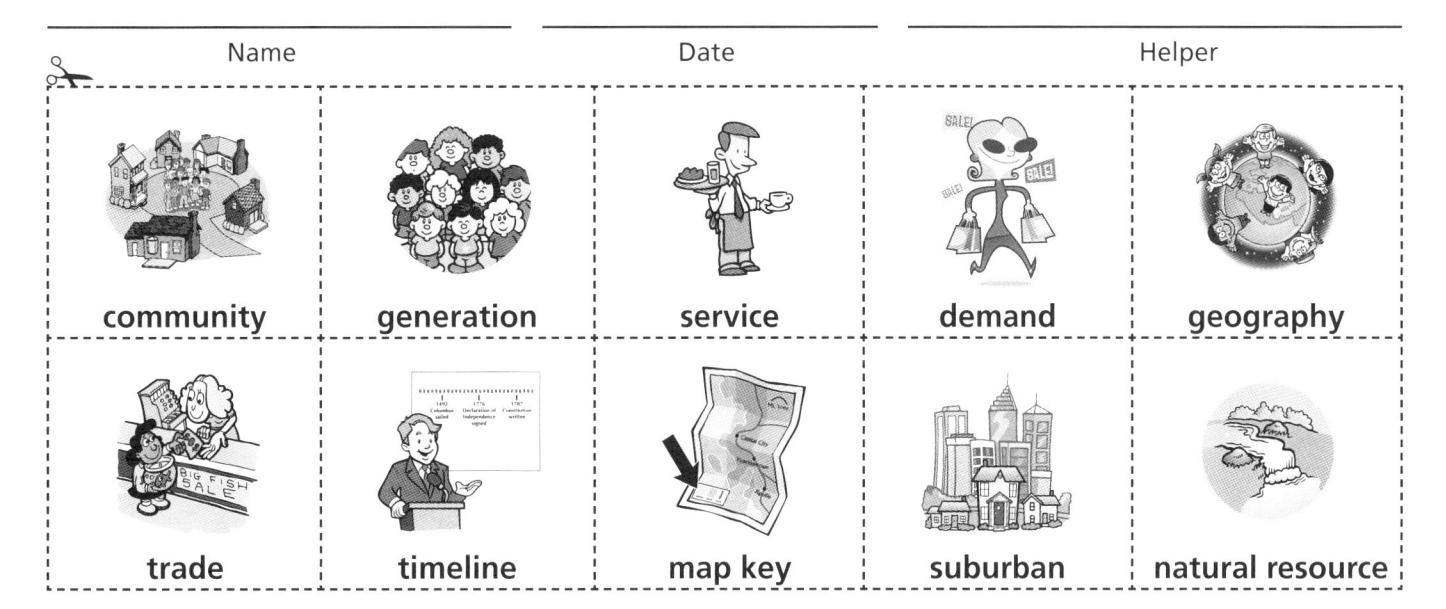

Name _____ Date _____ Helper _____

| community | generation | service | demand | geography |
| trade | timeline | map key | suburban | natural resource |

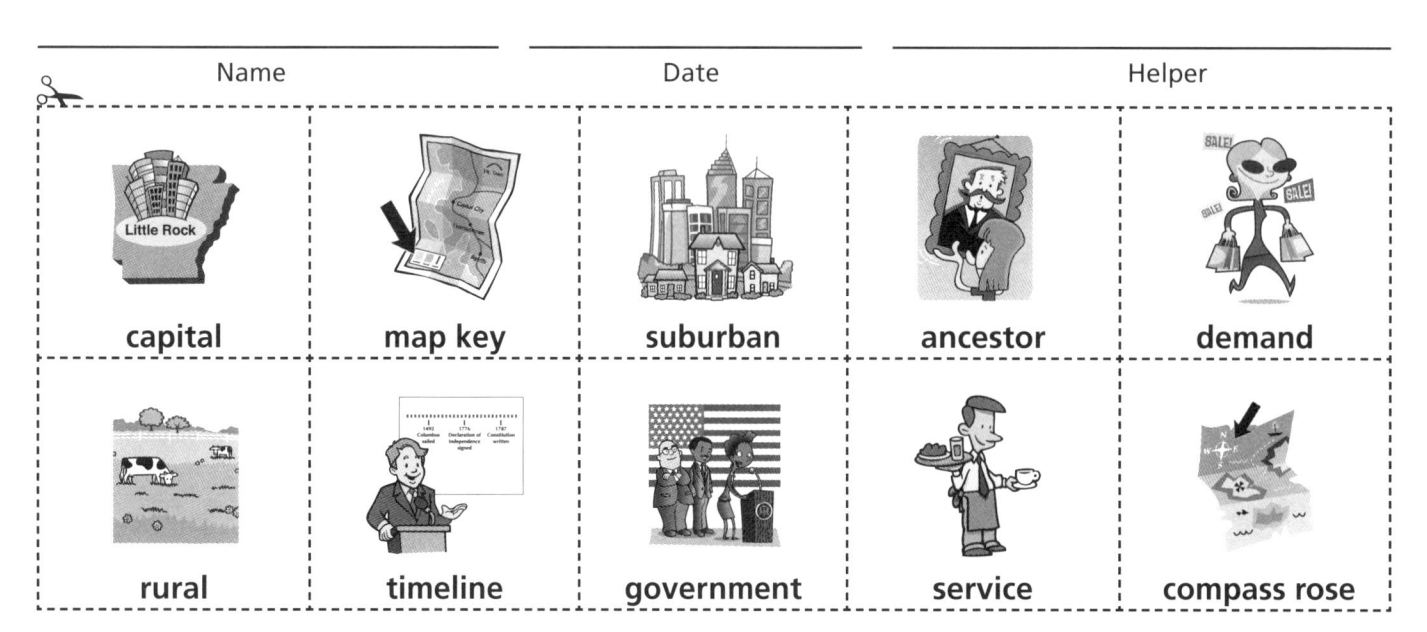

Social Studies – Breakdown

Directions: Have the students cut out the pictures. The student names each picture aloud and counts how many syllables (or parts of the word) it has. The student glues/tapes or places the picture on the side of the page with that number of syllables.

2 syllables	3 syllables

Name _____ Date _____ Helper _____

capital	map key	suburban	ancestor	demand
rural	timeline	government	service	compass rose

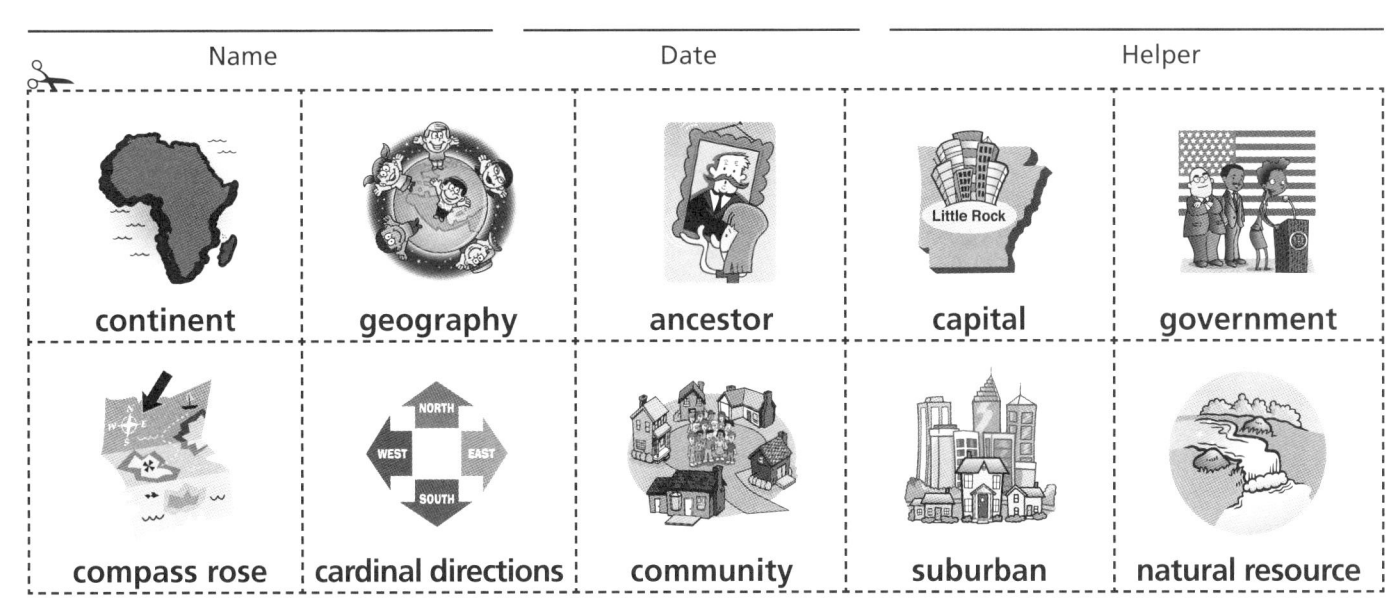

Social Studies – Syllable Search

Directions: Have the students cut out the pictures. The student names each picture aloud and counts how many syllables (or parts of the word) it has. The student glues/tapes or places the picture on the side of the page with that number of syllables. Have the student find the two words that don't belong and tell the number of syllables they have.

3 syllables	4 syllables

Name _____ Date _____ Helper _____

continent	geography	ancestor	capital	government
compass rose	cardinal directions	community	suburban	natural resource

Social Studies – Word Scramble Riddle

Directions: Unscramble the words to name each picture and write the letters in the blanks. Then take the letters in the circles and write them in order in the blanks at the bottom of the page to answer the riddle.

latnaur urceoser — __ __ t __ __ __ ⃝ __
__ __ s __ ⃝ __ __ __

adnlcria ietosdrcin — __ __ r __ ⃝ __
__ __ r ⃝ __ __ __ __ __

heoyggarp — __ __ __ __ __ __ ⃝ __

dneadm — __ __ m ⃝ ⃝ ⃝

lreade — __ __ __ ⃝ __ r

eemtiiln — __ ⃝ __ __ __ i __ ⃝

stecnaor — __ ⃝ __ __ s __ ⃝

What two things can you never eat for breakfast?

__ __ __ __ __ __ __ __ __ __ !

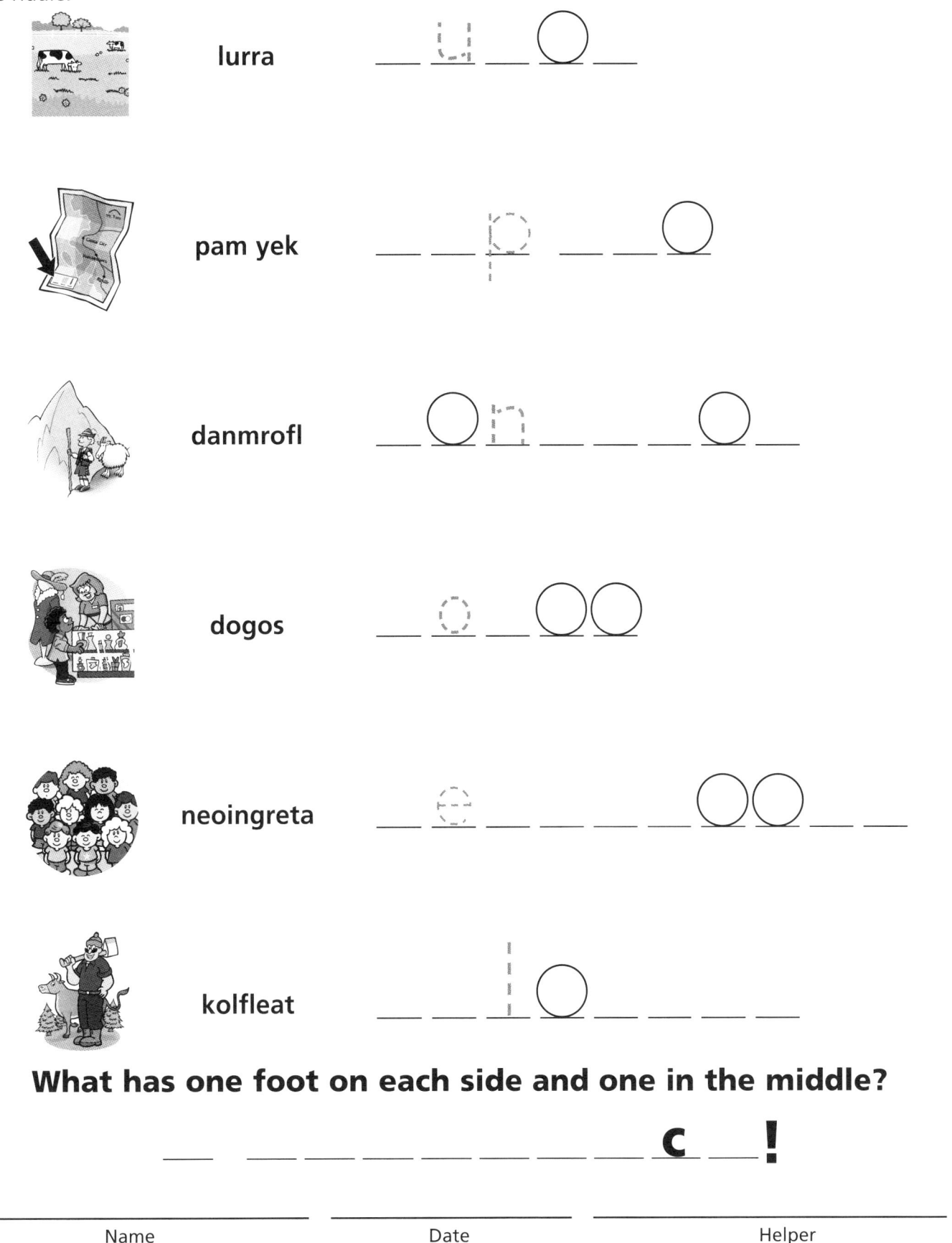

Social Studies – Word Scramble Riddle

Directions: Unscramble the words to name each picture and write the letters in the blanks. Then take the letters in the circles and write them in order in the blanks at the bottom of the page to answer the riddle.

lurra __ u __ ◯ __

pam yek __ __ p __ __ ◯

danmrofl ◯ n __ __ __ ◯ __

dogos __ o __ ◯◯

neoingreta __ e __ __ __ ◯◯ __ __

kolfleat __ __ __ i __ ◯ __ __ __

What has one foot on each side and one in the middle?

__ __ __ __ __ __ c __ !

Name   Date   Helper

Social Studies – Word Scramble Riddle

Directions: Unscramble the words to name each picture and write the letters in the blanks. Then take the letters in the circles and write them in order in the blanks at the bottom of the page to answer the riddle.

tentinnoc   _⃝_ _ _ _ n _⃝_ _

daret   _ _⃝_ d _

sapsomc sore   _ _ n _ _ _ _ ⃝⃝ _ _

nurba   _ _ b ⃝ _

daeelr   l _ _ ⃝ _ _

amp eyk   ⃝⃝⃝ k _ _

Where will you find roads without cars, forests without trees, and cities without houses?

___ ___ ___ ___ ___ ___ ___ ___ ___!

Social Studies – Writing Definitions

Directions: Read the vocabulary word below each picture. Then write a sentence beside each picture using the vocabulary word. Use the definition clues at the bottom of the page to help you.

1. **ancestor**

2. **culture**

3. **generation**

4. **folktale**

5. **goods**

6. **natural resource**

a group of people about the same age and growing up around the same time	things that are bought or sold	a made-up story that people have told over and over throughout the ages
something found in nature such as water, trees, and minerals that people need and use	a family member who lived before you did	shared beliefs and behaviors of a group of people

Name   Date   Helper

#BKCRD-56 Core Curriculum Vocab Cards Fun Sheets – Level 2 • ©2012 Super Duper® Publications • www.superduperinc.com

Social Studies – Writing Definitions

Directions: Read the vocabulary word below each picture. Then write a sentence beside each picture using the vocabulary word. Use the definition clues at the bottom of the page to help you.

1. **service**

2. **trade**

3. **supply**

4. **demand**

5. **cardinal directions**

6. **compass rose**

how many items are available for people to buy	buying and selling things	something that helps people or gives them what they want
a symbol on a map that shows north, south, east, and west	what you call north, south, east, and west	how much of something people want to buy

Name _____ Date _____ Helper _____

Social Studies – Writing Definitions

Directions: Read the vocabulary word below each picture. Then write a sentence beside each picture using the vocabulary word. Use the definition clues at the bottom of the page to help you.

1. continent

2. geography

3. urban

4. suburban

5. rural

6. community

something that has to do with the city	a group of people living in a particular place	a large area of land on Earth
something that has to do with the areas near a city where people live in houses	the study of the world's surface, its climate, and peoples	something that has to do with the countryside

Name   Date   Helper

Social Studies – Writing Definitions

Directions: Read the vocabulary word below each picture. Then write a sentence beside each picture using the vocabulary word. Use the definition clues at the bottom of the page to help you.

1. **region**

2. **landform**

3. **map key**

4. **capital**

5. **government**

6. **timeline**

a feature of the earth's surface such as a plain, mountain, or hill	a list that explains the meaning of the symbols and colors on a map	a display that shows when certain events happened over a period of time
the group of people who are in charge of a city, county, state, or country	a large area of a country or the world that has things in common	the main city in a state or country where government business takes place

Name Date Helper

Notes

Notes